Engineer Your Celebrity

How to Use Visibility Marketing to Stand Out from the Crowd and Achieve an Explosion of Growth for Your Business

Heather Ross

Engineer Your Celebrity: How to Use Visibility Marketing to Stand Out from the Crowd and Achieve an Explosion of Growth for Your Business

In association with:
Elite Online Publishing
63 E 11400 S #230
Sandy, UT 84070
EliteOnlinePublishing.com

ISBN: 978-1513655826

Table of Contents

Disclaimer

No guarantees are made to the amount of income you can make by following the suggestions in this book. You understand that each individual's success will be determined by multiple factors. This book is for information purposes only and is not intended to replace any legal advice or counsel. All examples in this book are solely examples and not intended to represent or guarantee that everyone will achieve the same results.

Introduction

I began my career by working in the field of marketing at corporate offices. However, working in big business never reaped any rewards for me. It was not a place that let my strengths shine, and I was bored. Office employment for me was just a place to bring home a salary, get the bills paid, invest in my retirement, and save for a vacation. Although I loved marketing, my jobs were just completing a daily routine and following instructions. I was never encouraged to give my thoughts and provide solutions, and no one had any interest in what I had to say or in finding out how I could contribute to the development of the department.

When I worked in the corporate world, I was told that I was too direct and that my "tell it like it is" straightforward approach would not get me very far in business. To succeed I had to soften my personality, sugarcoat my words, and slow down my fast-paced working style.

After I left the corporate world and became an entrepreneur, I discovered that customers who were working with me enjoyed my frankness and action-oriented work ethic. Business owners hire consultants because they want to be told what to do, and they want to see their support specialists as the problem solvers. It never occurred to me that my character traits and love of sharing ideas were a contributing factor to my success—until my clients began to praise my uniqueness.

That's what my goal is with this book. I'm telling it to you straight. I'm giving you point-blank strategies to use in the online world. I'm telling you directly what does and doesn't work. I hope that by being frank with you, I can make a difference, impact your life, contribute to your fulfilling your destiny, and help you build the business of your dreams. Over the years, the numerous people that I have worked with have seen tremendous progress in their businesses because of the tools that I implemented. I want to share these very same secrets in a direct manner so that they will transform you too.

Another reason for my launch into entrepreneurship is that I wanted more freedom than having to be in an office five days a week. I desired to travel; however, I didn't have a huge savings account, and I needed a full income. My boredom led me to spend time online researching options that would let me get out of my job and live the life I was seeking. So, after much research, I discovered the virtual industry of the internet marketing specialist.

What happened surprised me. I began to work with clients who valued my input and strategies. They loved the work I was doing and wanted my feedback for their projects and growth plans. Unlike in an office where they just assign you tasks and don't care about your ideas, small business clients do value you and do want to hear what you have to say. Being a virtual worker was life-changing and led to a complete transformation for me. It let me thrive. Working remotely increased my confidence because I could see all my capabilities and skills. I discovered talents that I didn't know I had.

In addition, I felt appreciated. In an office, you might receive an occasional thank you and a yearly bonus, but those don't give you a sense of being valued. Having my own business made me feel respected and empowered; it let me see that I am an intelligent human being who has a mark to make in the world. How amazing, motivating, and refreshing it is when your customers say thank you in their emails and phone calls or give you compliments such as "Great work; you are a genius!" Your esteem grows when clients pay your invoices each month, stick around, give you referrals, and sing your praises. I love being self-employed!

Also, working virtually allows me to create an independent lifestyle. I get to travel and go wherever I want—which I couldn't do with a nine-to-five. I can serve my clients anywhere—all I need is a laptop and an internet connection. It's true location freedom!

After a period of offering my services, I began to receive inquiries from entrepreneurs, such as coaches, authors, and speakers, who wanted to grow their online presence. They had heard about my expertise and turned to me to help grow their online profile and revenue in such areas as product orders, email subscribers, social media presence, and speaking engagements. I worked with people who had low followers on Instagram and Twitter, few likes on Facebook, email lists with only a few hundred people, and limited offers for speaking opportunities. By working with me, they significantly increased their online sales, lists, followers, and likes, and they got more speaking engagements.

I'm the type of person who uses patterns and plans to get things done. If a teacher explained something in school and I didn't get the lesson, I would come up with a different approach to learning the material and how to process the information. I did the same thing with my jobs. When I couldn't make sense of what the trainer was teaching, I would go figure it out on my own so I could get the work done.

When I became self-employed, I worked with many great clients. I noticed why some were successful and others weren't. I saw why some were catapulting their business and others were staying flat. The customers who were stuck and not growing their enterprises were using just traditional marketing and nothing more. The common denominator in the successful clients was that they were using both celebrity and traditional marketing.

The customers who used celebrity and traditional marketing used certain strategies to get the word out. My job as their internet marketing specialist was to set up content online; I saw which content would work in growing their online presence and lead to the sales chiming in and which content would not lead to any growth. I figured out what was and wasn't working and cracked the code of celebrity marketing. I created my own system and used it for my clients to become champions with their enterprises.

Because of my new abilities, I became a strategist in addition to offering my internet marketing specialist services. I would share my visibility tips with my customers and create strategic action plans with them. Those who used my methods would see enormous results and massive sales.

I know that you, the reader of this book, are an entrepreneur who will do what it takes to succeed and overcome any challenges that come your way. You went into business to make an impact and use your gifts to help others. You don't want to play small and just keep your head above the water—you want to leave an imprint. You understand that for the sales to come rolling in, you cannot just sit behind a desk, post now and then on social media, and send out some emails. You are looking to get out there and be visible in the online and off-line worlds to reap profits and rewards. You are looking for direction and the fertile seeds to create a visibility garden in your industry, to demonstrate your influence, and in turn to enable you to establish a profit-making client magnet brand.

I believe that anyone who wants to create a prominent presence and showcase their expertise in their field to attract a client base that needs their services should be able to do so. That's why I have written this book.

With this book, I'm sharing with you the practical business building tools that led my clients to an explosion of opportunity with their businesses and online success. I'm giving out the secrets that I use as a strategist with my customers for them to achieve massive followers online, become sought-after speakers, and reach profits over the six-figure mark. I am passionate about helping and motivating entrepreneurs to discover their passion, stand out as thought leaders, and crack the six-figure code to build the business of their dreams. I want you to achieve the same boost in your business as my clients did, for you to make your mark on the world. It's time to be the empowered entrepreneur you were born to be.

FREE GIFT

Engineer Your Celebrity Productivity Planner

To thank you for purchasing my book, I have a special gift for you!

A free electronic productivity planner where you can put together your to-do list and action items as you select the components of the celebrity marketing mix and build your business as an industry leader.

To get you closer to achieving your goals, included in the planner are the components of each mix, and tips with advice.

http://www.HeatherRossMarketing.com/celebrity-planner

ADDITIONAL GIVEAWAYS

7 Surefire Infusionsoft Strategies to Grow Your List 10X. Get Ready to Have a Huge List That Has Low Unsubscribes and Produces High Paying Clients

Content Marketing Explained: Why Your Business Needs Content. Get your e-book with everything you need to know about content marketing.

New items are always being added so keep checking back at the website.

http://www.HeatherRossMarketing.com/free-stuff

COMPLIMENTARY SESSION AND WORK WITH HEATHER

30 minute "Business Breakthrough" coaching session.
We'll work together to...
- Create a crystal clear vision for your "ultimate business success" and the "perfect lifestyle" you'd like your business to provide
- Uncover hidden challenges that may be sabotaging the growth of your business and keeping you working too many hours
- Leave this session renewed, re-energized, and inspired to turn your business into a highly profitable, revenue-generating machine that practically runs itself.
http://www.HeatherRossMarketing.com/complimentary-session

CONNECT WITH HEATHER

- Connect with Heather on Facebook
http://www.HeatherRossMarketing.com/facebook
- Connect with Heather on LinkedIn
http://www.HeatherRossMarketing.com/linkedin
- Connect with Heather on Twitter
http://www.HeatherRossMarketing.com/twitter
- For more free business building tips and additional information about Heather, go to
http://www.HeatherRossMarketing.com

Chapter One
Mind-set

Do What Must Be Done to Be a Success

Let me tell it to you straight—the difference between the people who succeed in achieving massive profits with their businesses and the ones who don't is mind-set. The people who have the motivation and mind-set that they will do what it takes for success are the ones who become the superstars. Those who stick to their plans and don't give up are the ones who are still around in the future. The ones who succumb to their fears and limiting beliefs—who say they can't do it, it won't work, and it's a waste of time—don't go anywhere.

That's not to say that you don't have the right mind-set if you feel a strategy won't work for you. If you feel that something doesn't apply to your business and are going to research another avenue that you think will suit your needs more, that's perfect. That's having the mind-set of looking for what you feel is suitable for your company and will work for you. However, saying you won't be a success or closing your mind to most strategies won't lead you anywhere.

Throughout this book, I'm going to talk about how you should not be afraid to share your triumphs with your audience.

Share Your Accomplishments

Most people don't want to show off, as we were told from our early youth that no one likes a show-off. However, if you want people rushing to work with you, you need to show off, and there is no shame in doing so. You have come far in life, and it's time to let others know. No one is going to have a low opinion of you for talking about your achievements; they understand that you have accomplished something and are telling people because that is how business works. They will be impressed that you are being transparent and have the courage to get out there, make life-changing decisions, and not hide behind a desk. If you are afraid of letting others know about your achievements, then you must break the chains you are in and free yourself to become someone who gets out there and toots their own horn.

If you want this book to work for you, you must have the mind-set that you want to share your success. You are proud of your accomplishments, and you want others to know. You understand that the way to get customers to hire you is to share your achievements. You will not be afraid, you will not let others intimidate you, you will ignore the naysayers, and you will get out there. Get those speaking opportunities, and afterward post online about the places you have spoken at. I want to motivate you to develop this empowering mind-set because it will benefit you tremendously.

Be Persistent

Another area that I will bring up many times is persistence. You can't just do something a few times and then give up because you don't see instant results. The mind-set that you must have to run a highly lucrative business is persistence. It takes time for marketing to work. Although many gurus and people will tell you that they applied some concepts and got overnight success, I'm not going to tell you this will occur. I've worked with numerous people over the years who have achieved enormous victories. However, none of them saw this happen because they did one thing one time and *boom*, the money came rolling it. They made huge profits only because they applied a technique over a period and then continued to apply the technique. Only after continuous hard work did the proceeds arrive.

You can't give up and be insecure, as there will be many down periods, especially when first starting out. When you launch a business, you will get many no's before a yes, and it takes time for a business to bear fruit. Even when you first start getting yeses, there will still be many people who have no interest in working with you. The important thing is to keep going.

Continually Repeat and Recycle Content

Use this book as a guide to have the business of your dreams and have the mind-set to not give up. You will continually write about your speaking opportunities and discuss your educational content with your audience. If some of the posts you put out online don't give any returns, you will not walk away but will post again and again. You will evaluate why the post did not get the returns you wanted, adjust the writing style, wait some time for the post to no longer be fresh in people's minds, and post it again. Giving up is not an option. You must have the mind-set that you must continually put together content and will stay motivated to repeat and recycle the content for as many people as possible to find out about you.

Transform yourself to have these empowering mind-sets—doing what it takes, sharing your story, being persistent, and repeating content—and you will be on your way to achieving your destiny with a business that flourishes.

Recap

The four mind-sets of a prosperous business owner:
- Do what must be done to be a success.
- Share your accomplishments.
- Be persistent.
- Continually repeat and recycle content.

Chapter Two

The Psychology of Marketing

Many studies discuss the psychological reasons why people purchase. Many of the reasons people take out their wallets and purchase are status, power, popularity, income growth, and escape from the rigors of the daily world. Advertising is built around promises that ordering a specific product will fulfill your wants and needs. Marketing messages are all about the promise of what the product can do for you, and that's not to mention the loads of hidden messages in ads that make you buy a product whether you are aware of your motivation or not.

Advertising also uses repetition. Ads repeat their messages many times on television, on the internet, and in print. A person who watches, reads, and hears an ad at numerous intervals will in the end believe it and finally proceed to the cash register.

While I don't support using hidden messages or promising people fictional advantages, there are some advertising concepts that I do encourage and believe you need to use to effectively get the word out about your company. They are status and repetition.

Status

Let's start with status. Status means that you are a leader, expert, and influencer in your industry. Status signals to people that you are who you say you are and that you can deliver on your promise. People buy because of status, whether they admit it or not. If you can demonstrate to others that you are a success—someone of importance—people will want to do business with you. Let's be clear here: you are not telling people that you are a cool person and fun to spend time around; rather, you are telling the audience that the solutions you promise them do work. You implemented those solutions in your business, and they took you to where you are now. Who are you now? An entrepreneur of enormous success who is sharing your secrets with them, and these secrets will give them the same results.

Let's set the scene here with two people: Person A and Person B.

Person A tells you that they have used their strategies to build a million-dollar company. They show you a nice house, awesome vacations, a roster of speaking engagements, images of them delivering keynote talks in front of roomfuls of people, book titles with the words Amazon best seller, and so on.

Person B tells you they are a success, but you never see them anywhere. They have never written a book and have just a few followers on social media. Maybe they have spoken at events, but you never see any images. Perhaps they have appeared on podcasts, but they never share the links.

Who would you purchase from? Take a moment to think about it based on the information above.

It could be that Person A does not in reality have great strategies of success. For all you know, their house and vacations are paid with an inheritance, and the photo of them in a room filled with people was taken years ago when they gave a speech for a company they were employed with and had not yet launched their business.

Person B might have great strategies and really know their material. Maybe they have spoken at several places, and lots of people attend their events and love their speeches.

You, though—the observer of person A and B—are not going to think that Person B is a success who is just not very good at tooting their horn. You are going to assume the more successful person is person A, and whether that is a fair assumption to make is irrelevant. That's just the way it is. Perception is reality in the online domain.

If you want to be a success online in today's world, you have to set yourself up to be as visible as person A. Accept it and don't argue about it.

Person A is going to be the one who gets the sales and grows their business. Person B is not going anywhere online and is just deadwood. I'm not saying that Person B won't make some money. They might get customers from in-person meetings, and maybe they will go to networking events and give inspiring elevator speeches and get referrals. However, no one is going to be impressed with their social media pages and websites, and few sales are going to come from online marketing. Person B might know how to get some sales with off-line activities—but this book is not about partaking in just a few off-line activities; this book is how to be a mega sensation to boost your profits by combining both off-line and online strategies to the maximum.

Person A will be the one who gets the online sales. Also, when Person A goes to networking events, they will get more sales than Person B ever could. Think of how amazing they will be at networking if they mention they appeared on a radio show or show samples of their book at a vendor booth. Think of the difference of perception when someone meets both A and B at an event. What happens when the new associate goes to their smartphone to check out Person A's and Person B's websites and social media pages?

They see moving content on Person A's pages but nothing stirring on Person B's pages. Most people don't go and buy after meeting someone for three minutes. Instead, they check them out online—either on their phone at the event or after when they arrive home. Whom will they be more awestruck by?

Many people believe that social media results in direct sales. It doesn't. Social media achieves two things. First, it maintains connection. What often happens is that a colleague meets you at a business forum and takes an interest in your presentation or is wowed by your elevator speech. However, they most likely don't need your services right away. Because you have read this book and follow the advice in its pages, you decide to friend them on Facebook and connect with them on LinkedIn. They are now in your inner circle of business associates.

The second thing that social media achieves is that it sways people to want to work with you. Over the next several months, that new person in your inner online circle is now following you and continues to be dumbfounded with you as they are reading superb content on your social media pages. Over time they develop confidence in working with you. When the moment comes that the colleague is looking for the services you offer, they call you up for a discussion because you are at the top of their mind.

Not everyone who is impressed with you and follows you online is going to connect with you in the future. However, the more people you have in your channels, the more likely there will be people who do make that phone call. This is the leverage of social media. It's not automatic. It's a long-term strategy.

Look at social media and your website as ways for someone to research you. If a prospective client is considering hiring you but knows nothing about you, they are going to research you. There are two ways they can do the research: they can ask around for references, or they can check you out online. To get associates to say electrifying things about you means that you must do a superb job for each client. For the online portion, it means that you provide rich, saucy content.

Now let's talk about that content. What makes people want to work with you over someone else who offers something similar to your business? It's back to that magical word we spoke about at the introduction to this chapter: status. When someone reads your social media posts, your free e-book, and your blog posts, they see great substance and visuals. In addition to the free tips that you provide, you are also sharing with them your status (speaking events, radio show appearances, etc.). They see you are someone of importance who knows what you are talking about and is invited everywhere to share their mastery, and that is what is going to motivate them to work with you.

You are writing a blog and social media posts filled with great business advice and strategies that readers want to implement in their own businesses. Even more amazing is that you are sharing speaking engagements and pictures of events you attend and are talking about how the book you wrote is a best seller. The viewer sees that you can get in front of audiences, that people are inviting you to speak, and that the comments on your blog pages and Amazon book pages are discussions by readers of your books and blog posts. It shows your status, leadership, and expertise—you are truly generating buzz for your business.

Take a moment now and go look online at a leader in your industry that you admire. Look at how client attraction works for them. What are they saying and doing online? You will see they are using the marketing tool of status, and that is what is making you want to work with them.

Marketing is about promises—usually greater income and success. By sharing with your audience your stories of prominence, you are sending the message of how to achieve success. You are telling them that they can achieve the success you have achieved if they follow your tips, programs, and strategies.

Repetition

Repetition is key. Don't mention something just once. Mention it many, many, many times. If your article appeared in a prestigious magazine, don't post it once on social media and then forget about it. Post on your pages every two months over the next two to three years that your article appeared in this magazine. Write a blog post about it, mention it in your bio, send out a newsletter about it, and then mention it again in your newsletter six months later. Not everyone sees the social media post for the first time. If they missed your post the first time around, they will most likely see it when it goes out again. If they are new to your community, they might not see it the first three times it went out, but they will see it the fourth or fifth time.

If you think that you will be inundating your followers who do read your content by continually repeating the same thing, you won't be. Don't say the same thing every day or every week. However, don't worry that in two to six months people will remember prior content; people are bombarded with loads of information daily and likely won't remember something from a few months ago. Give your content a boost, and share it again and again and again. Don't be afraid, and repeat, repeat, repeat.

Repeating content many times ensures that as many people as possible get to find out about your achievements and remember your triumphs.

I hope that I have demonstrated to you the importance of status and repetition. Before you continue reading this book, you must understand these two areas, as they are the foundation for everything that follows. If you accept these two concepts, then the rest of the book will be easy for you; everything that follows simply ties in.

Recap

- To achieve status online, continually share your stories of your triumphs.
- Talk about your best-selling book, and post pictures of your speaking appearances and of the networking functions you attend.
- Mention your successes many, many, many times. Post them online, and then revisit them every two months for the next two to three years.
- The purpose of social media is not direct sales. Social media is about maintaining a connection with your audience and having them develop confidence in your abilities as they get to know you.

Chapter Three

Marketing

Simply put, marketing is getting the word out to the marketplace. It comprises the tools to get the word out, the process of reaching out to and communicating with your target audience, and the dialogue that will make your readers and listeners want to pick up the phone to purchase from you.

Getting the Word Out

If we start with the first part of the definition, marketing comprises the tools to get the word out.

Here is the arsenal of strategies you might use to get the word out—the marketing mix:

- Websites
- Social media
- Giveaways

- Newsletters
- Blog posts
- Articles
- Podcasts
- Speaking engagements
- Networking events
- Business cards
- Booths at conferences
- Symposium sponsorships
- Telesummit appearances

This marketing mix is where you invest time and money. While you don't need to be doing everything I listed, you do need to be doing a lot of it to have a successful business.

You need to be working on your selected components of the marketing mix on a regular basis. If you decide to have a Facebook page for your marketing, don't post once a month—you need to post on the page at least once a day. If you are using public speaking to attract clientele, you need to be speaking several times a month and not just once every six months.

Make sure to have a deep understanding of each element of the marketing mix that you choose to work on. Take the time to learn each of them, how they work, and how they can be utilized for the advancement of your business visibility.

Let's take public speaking, for example. Many times people just email networking groups and ask to speak at their next meeting. However, most networking groups give these speaking slots to members over nonmembers. Thus, a great way to get speaking opportunities is to be a member of several networking groups. At first, most chapters will want you to attend events where you just network and don't present on stage. Once they get to know you, they then let you get on the stage.

The bottom line is that marketing is consistently using the marketing mix elements. Understand what each component involves, and put together a strategic vision plan for how to tackle it. Don't make assumptions, and do your research. Taking the time to tackle the marketing mix properly will give you the desired results that will drive your business forward.

What Are You Saying to Your Audience?

The next part of the marketing definition is that marketing is communicating with your audience. What are you saying to them?

When people think of marketing, they think promotion: advertising your prices, your services, and what you can do for a prospect. While this part is all true, let's take a step back before we investigate advertising and instead add another area to marketing—education.

Education

Education is a key approach to communicating with your target audience. Educational and promotional content compose the dialogue with your audience and will appear in the different elements of the marketing arsenal.

The education part of marketing involves the tips and resources you are giving away to people for free. Yes, that's correct. Free!

When you go to an ice cream shop, they let you sample a bit of the ice cream for no charge (e.g., Baskin-Robbins's pink spoon). The idea is that you will like the free sample and proceed to order a carton.

It's the same with your company. You'll give away plenty of free information with the intent that your audience will love what you have to say and then will desire more.

Here's how it's done. Create free e-books, give great speeches, and write blog posts that have relevant information that your target market needs to learn. Talk, talk, talk and write, write, write. Of course, you won't give everything away for free. To receive the next level of information, the customers will have to pay for it. The high-end content and secrets will be locked away and can only be accessed with a credit card.

Promotion

Now back to promotion. Promotion involves letting your audience know about your products and services and what you have to offer. First, you educate the listener, and then you let them know about the sale.

At the end of your speech, take a few minutes to let the audience know how they can reach you for your services, or at the end of your free e-book, mention some more resources that might be of interest to them, and provide the link that leads to a sales page where they can go to purchase these resources. Now that they are full of knowledge about you, many people will want to hire you. Of course, not everyone will hire you, which is why again you must always be getting out there and connecting with more people. The more people you encounter, the bigger the impact you will have.

The rule of thumb that people follow is called the 80-20 rule. If you are posting on social media, 80 percent is free educational content while 20 percent is promotional. If you are giving a speech, the majority is educational while the last bit is promotional.

Target Audience

Remember, marketing is communicating. To communicate effectively, you need to have a good understanding of your audience. Investigate who will need your services and what problem you solve for them. Narrow in on your audience: their age, location, gender, marital status, type of business, financial income, and so on. Not all of these will apply to you (you might not care about their marital status, for example). However, many will. To get a snapshot, take some time and write down a description or list of what your target audience looks like.

To have a good understanding of your audience, you might want to consult market research studies. You can either do your own market research by hiring an agency (very expensive) or you can purchase paid studies (pricey but not as expensive as hiring an agency for your own unique study). To find paid studies that are already complete, google "find market studies," and search from there. Purchase some reports, and read them to get a good grasp and clear picture of your audience.

To communicate with your target market, determine where they hang out. Join their networking groups, take part in their Facebook groups, attend the symposiums they attend, and promote your giveaways on the websites they frequent.

Very often it takes time to find the exact places your target audience hangs out. When I opened my business, I knew that I needed to go to networking groups to get clients. However, I did not know the right ones to join. Many networking organizations don't require you to join right away, and they let you attend usually two meetings as a nonmember. You are not required to pay for the membership, just the fee for the event. (The event fee for nonmembers is usually a few dollars more than the price members pay.)

Here's what I did. As an internet marketing specialist, my target market was women who were self-employed as coaches, authors, or speakers and were looking for someone to assist them virtually for around ten to twenty hours a month. I googled the networking groups in my city and researched their websites. Based on the information that came up, I chose three networking groups that looked like they would meet my business needs and signed up for their events.

I attended the events one or two times for each group. I spoke to the people in the room and checked out the members' websites. Based on my conversations and the types of businesses that the members owned, I chose the networking group that matched my interests the most, paid for a yearly membership, and made it a point to attend an event once or twice a month to build my customer database. I also joined their Facebook group and their online discussion forum.

Once I successfully set myself up as a member of this networking group online and off-line, I looked for a second networking group to join using the same process.

Getting a clear picture of your audience and spending time in the places that they are present will enable you to be a heartfelt communicator with your target market.

Your target market is a segment of the overall population. You are a small business owner, and you don't have to market to the whole country to be successful. You are not Coca-Cola or Best Buy, who target everyone. Make sure to not fall into the trap of comparing yourself to big businesses that target huge groups of people. It's okay to exclude segments, and you will still be successful.

The basic rule with target marketing is that if you're marketing to everyone, you're marketing to no one. Don't fall into this trap, and do take the time to discover your target market.

When you have a good understanding of your target market, you will be able to create the right educational and promotional campaigns to reach them. A business owner who communicates using the right language with their market will see the market respond with positive revenue results.

Planting the Seed

The results from networking and social media are not instantaneous. You might introduce yourself to someone at a networking event who is impressed with your elevator speech but doesn't need your services now. However, that does not mean they won't need them later. If you keep connecting with them at your monthly chapter meetings, then you will be top of mind when they do need your expertise.

Having giveaways, speaking at events, and connecting at business functions to let people know how spectacular you are is called planting the seed. Your audience will not need your services right away, but many will need your services in the future. When they do, you will be top of mind because you gave great free information to them at some point. You planted the seed with some free educational content and watered the seed by staying in touch with them on social media and frequently attending local group meetings. When they do need your product, the plant is ready to be harvested.

Many times entrepreneurs I work with who are new to the networking world tell me how they attended an event and did not find anyone to work with. When they tell me this, I then proceed to check with them that they handed out their business cards to attendees, mentioned their irresistible free offers, and connected with the attendees on social media. I let them know that they did all the necessary steps, and now they just need to make sure to attend future chapter events and to focus on the rest of the marketing mix. What often happens is that the entrepreneurs who were disappointed that they did not get customers from the first few events they attended are now receiving phone calls months later from the people they met at these first few events. The bottom line is it takes time for networking events to bear fruit; you must be patient and just keep watering the field of your planted seeds.

Establish Connections and Form Relationships

Always show up each month to networking meetings looking and talking your best. Be friendly and professional, and never discount someone based on a job title or type of business they operate. When you see them again at the next meeting, make sure to walk over and give a friendly hello and ask how things are going for them. Perhaps this chapter member will never need your service, but you could be first of mind as a referral when someone asks them for a recommendation. Or maybe they will be hosting an event and will need a speaker that just happens to be for an area that you specialize in.

I learned this concept when I managed a coach's successful podcast for years. When I went to the events for the chapters that I belonged to, many times I did not need member services, and they did not need mine. However, if a colleague was the right fit for the podcast, I invited them to be a guest on the show.

The same goes for your giveaways. If you follow my advice, then you are someone who will create a great gift with fabulous educational info, and at each networking function, you will invite the members to check out your website, sign up for your gift, and contact you for your services. Members might not need your services now, but if they signed up for your freebie, you will still easily stay in contact with them and thus continue to maintain the newly formed connection.

How did those people sign up for the free offer? You asked for their email address. To follow spam rules, ask for their email address to sign up for your newsletter, and inform them that by signing up for your newsletter, you will give them a gift as a thank you. They are now on your email list. You will be communicating with them on a regular basis with emails that are full of valuable information and, occasionally, sales. As you are creating a relationship with them, they will turn to you when they need your expertise.

You Are the Expert

The last part of the marketing definition is that the dialogue (content) will make your readers and listeners want to pick up the phone to purchase from you.

What makes someone want to purchase from you? The answer is that you provide a product or service that gives a solution to their needs. However, what makes them purchase from you and not the competition? Why should they choose you as the one to solve their dilemma? The answer is that you are the expert in your industry.

You've given people the materials and engaged with them in person and through your social media and emails. You've provided rich, heartfelt, valuable content and your unique special sauce. You are the savant in your field, and when they need an adept entrepreneur, they will turn to you.

Someone who is considering doing business with you is going to first check you out. They might have read a few emails or heard your elevator speech at an event that piqued their interest. Next, they will check out your website, read some blog posts, look at your social media pages, and listen to your podcasts. If you don't have anywhere for them to check you out, how will they know you are the one to hire? If when they check you out, they see poor quality, they will change their minds.

That's why the free material you provide can't be of low quality. While you for sure want to keep some of your great information locked away for paying customers, you must make it a point that anything you do for free is of great quality. Otherwise, you won't be seen as proficient, and no one will want to do business with you.

Show Off

Social media, email marketing, and websites turn the owners of these pages into celebrities; they become famous to their followers. It's now time to take advantage of your newfound celebrity and show it off to your fans.

When you have a speaking event, are on a podcast, or appear on a telesummit, let your peeps know. There's no point in being a guest on a podcast if you are not going to share it with people. Perhaps the listeners of the podcast you appeared on have no need for your services; however, someone who stops by your Facebook page or blog and reads how you were invited to be a guest on a show is going to be impressed. I have seen many times people speak at places and don't share it. Big mistake. I don't quite understand why they are hiding it. They should be proud of their accomplishments.

When you go to an event, share the photos of the event the next day. Show the pictures of yourself at a podium speaking in front of people, and show the snapshots of you engaging with the audience. Again, it's impressive; therefore, write blog posts about it, and let your social media fans and email readers know. Just get the word out and be a show-off. Why wouldn't you want to show off? You just achieved something—celebrate! Communicate that you are the expert and what an awesome person you are. Only by doing so will you be seen as an influencer in your industry.

WIIFT—What's in It for Them?

People buy from people who will help them solve a problem and achieve results for their business. They will take promotional materials seriously if you let them know that by purchasing this product, they will achieve a result. Always keep this in mind. It's not about you—it's about the target audience. When designing your materials, always ask, "What's in it for them?"

For example, when making a presentation to your audience, don't say, "I have been in business for eight years." Say, "I'm sharing with you that I've been in business for eight years because I want you to be assured that I will deliver that same superb quality service that has kept me in business for this long." It's okay to point out the WIIFT. Don't assume your audience will make the connection.

Everything you do and everything you approach should always be answering WIIFT. Every blog post you write, every presentation you give, every elevator speech you make—they always must answer that question. That should be your focus. How do you remember to keep the focus on WIIFT? You prepare everything. It's easy to get distracted and forget this concept because you have so much you want to say. You want them to know how experienced you are and make sure they get all the information to learn your important topic. However, make the "about you" part secondary. The additional information that might not apply to their business has to be kept short. That's not to say that extra educational and biographical material in your blog or speech should be removed. If you feel it is needed, then keep it. Just make it short.

Later on in this book in chapters "Where to Speak Online" and "Where to Speak in Person," I will discuss how to post photos of your speaking appearances in your presentations, social media, websites, and emails. People are visual, and showing photos of your achievements answers the WIIFT—they see you are a success, so they trust that by working with you and following you, they too can become a success. The photos inspire prospects and give them the courage that they can achieve the results that you have achieved if they decide to work with you.

Recap

- Marketing is getting the word out to the marketplace.
- The marketing mix comprises the tools you use to get the word out.
- The marketing dialogue with your target audience involves both educational and promotional content.
- Expertise is a big factor in purchasing decisions.
- Marketing is consistently using the marketing mix.
- Follow the 80-20 rule.
- Always ask, "What's in it for them?"
- If you're marketing to everyone, you're marketing to no one.
- Sales are not immediate. You need to develop relationships.
- Show off your speaking success.

Chapter Four

Branding

Once you've decided which marketing materials you need, it's time to design everything. You want your materials to look professional, consistent, and clear so that your marketing message is easily understood. This step is where branding comes into place.

Branding is the message of who you are and always answers the question of why someone should do business with you; it lets your prospects know that you are the company that can deliver the results they need. By having that consistent feel and message, your audience will take you seriously and grasp why you are the one to do business with. Brands enhance not only your confidence as a business owner but also the confidence in the consumers that you really can deliver what you promise.

Branding is the specific look that all your materials will have. That look is a certain visual appearance that provides an image and message of what your business is all about.

When your materials have the right design, your audience will take you seriously and understand what you are all about. Branding gives you that special mojo to set you apart from the competition.

Branding is what customers perceive of your company. Your brand is the promise that you intend to make to the customers. The ultimate goal is to spark a connection, create a positive feeling, and get loyalty to a specific product from purchasers.

Focus on the Client, Not You

One thing that usually happens when setting up a brand is that the focus is all on the company owner. This approach is not the one to take. Doing branding properly means you need to focus on your target market—potential and current customers.

You want good branding to show that you are professional and to be taken seriously. You want to show your personality and thus attract the right type of people to work with. However, you don't want to get lost in making everything about you. People do not buy from you because you have a nice personality and are a fun person; they buy from someone who can help them and solve a problem. It's not about you—it's about them. People buy from companies that deliver results to their problems and enhance the quality of their life. When working on your branding, keep asking, "What's in it for them?" (WIIFT).

It's fine to talk about you, share your story, and choose colors and fonts that you like. Just make sure they apply to your audience. Proper branding provides your target audience the opportunity to learn about you and form a connection that will lead to them working with you.

A perfect example is your website's "About" page. You want to share a bit of your story because it shows people your experience, the clients you've worked with, whether you've appeared on any radio shows, and so on. Just don't get carried away and make it all about you with nothing relevant to the reader. Most likely your story is how you started your business from the bottom and are now a success or how you discovered some formula that led to a better and more efficient way of doing things. Your message in your biography is to illustrate to the reader that you were able to achieve something and that they too can achieve it by partnering with you. Sharing your story is about the reader being inspired to want to work with you and gaining confidence in you because of your experience. It lets the reader develop trust in you.

Branding Components

- Logo
- Tagline
- Colors
- Fonts
- Message
- Your uniqueness
- Your style

These components will be part of your website, brochures, PowerPoint presentations, and social media pages, and they will always stay the same. Consistency matters. Consistent branding means your audience understands what you have to offer and will easily remember what you are all about. It also demonstrates your professionalism.

Message

As we discussed in the beginning of this chapter, branding is the message of who you are and always answers the question of why someone should do business with you. Your message includes how you provide a product or a service that delivers results—WIIFT.

When deciding on your message, ask yourself the following questions:

- What message do you want to send to your audience?
- What makes you different?
- What are you about?
- What are you trying to tell your customers?
- What visual look do you want your marketing materials to have?
- What do you want your customers to feel when they see your materials?
- What are the results that you deliver to your customers?
- Why are you the company that can provide the results?
- What is the reason that someone should buy from you?

Make sure that before you answer these questions that you know who your target market is. Without a good understanding of your target audience, you won't be able to answer these questions and set up a message that will make you a client attraction machine.

Fonts and Colors

Based on your style and target market, choose fonts and colors for your branding that reflect your message and what you're about. Focus on the fonts and colors that fit with your target market, and spend time researching the different meanings in the color wheel.

If a certain color applies to your target audience, then this can be your brand color. For example, if you're a positivity speaker, then choose colors that reflect warmth and happiness, such as orange, yellow, or red. If your audience is primarily women, then the colors you might want are pink or purple.

Logos

A logo is necessary because it makes your business look professional and adds consistency; you'll put the logo on most of your materials. A logo gives a business a look and feel and makes people form a connection with the company. Your goal in branding is to create an image that has a positive emotional impact with people. A company with a logo versus a company that does not have one comes across as a more credible place to shop from.

You should definitely take the time to design a great-looking logo for all these reasons. However, take note: logos are not going to get you sales, and no one buys a product or hires someone because the logo is cool or professionally designed.

Consumers of small businesses buy from the person behind the company and not the logo. So, while I for sure agree that you must put your logo on your marketing materials, that alone does not accomplish anything. You still must let your audience know all about you. You need your bio on your website, your photo on your Facebook business page, and speaking engagements on your roster.

Many small business owners are very timid in showing their faces. They create websites and Facebook pages without their photo yet spend all their time making sure there is a logo on their marketing materials. Too many times I have seen business owners put their logo on their Facebook page profile image and header—with no photo of them anywhere to be found. The lack of their photo is a major mistake. Here's what I instruct them to do and will now instruct you—put your logo in the Facebook header section, and put your photo in the profile image section. Better yet, for the header section, put your logo combined with your photo and tagline. A logo, tagline, and personal photo send the message to the readers of the page that you are a professional company, and they will want to read the page to learn more about you.

As so many people get wrapped up in their logo, I'm going to repeat it: consumers buy from you and not your logo.

Tagline

A tagline is a quick summary of what you can do for your customers. It's taken from your message, is catchy and simple, and should connect with a prospect right away so they get you and understand you. The tagline forms an impact and makes a promise of what you are going to deliver.

A proper tagline sums up which results you can deliver. Whatever your tagline is, it answers the question WIIFT. Although we often think that a tagline needs to be catchy, it needs to also answer how you can help your audience and provide solutions for them.

The tagline is placed on the cover of your brochures and the headers of your website and Facebook page. It goes in a clearly visible place so that the reader can immediately grasp what you are all about. In today's world, everything is instantaneous. Although a person will understand your company once they read your web pages and brochures, you can't assume that someone is going to take the time to do all that reading—you need to catch their attention right away. If you catch their attention, then they will go ahead and read about you. However, if you don't catch their interest, they'll just drop the brochure somewhere or move on to another website.

When I started out in business as a virtual support specialist in marketing, my tagline was "Online Marketing Solutions to Grow Your Business." When I moved into specializing in Infusionsoft and marketing, my tagline was "The Right Marketing . . . Relevant and Automated!"

Who Are You? What Is Your Personality? What Is Your Style?

As I said above, logos do not get you sales. If you are a small business owner, then you are not a large company like IBM or Pepsi. You are the face of your business, and you need to get out there.

Remember, throughout your marketing mix, you need to display your pictures and tell your stories. People buy from the person behind the business.

Who you are and your personality have a lot to do with your brand. So, when designing your brand, take some time to look at yourself—that insight will form part of the message in communicating with people.

We've looked at how branding answers what makes you different from competitors. One thing that a competing business does not have is you—talk about you, and let consumers see your uniqueness and your special style of service. As Simon Mainwaring (a Global Thought Leader on Branding) said, "The keys to brand success are self-definition, transparency, authenticity, and accountability."

Look at your traits, and include them in your branding message. For example, I am direct, fast-paced, and reliable, and I love marketing. As an authentic entrepreneur, I always mention these traits. You'll find them on my website "About" page and in testimonials from customers. I don't hide from these behaviors; I am proud of them and always let people know about them. There are plenty of people out there who don't want to work with someone who has a direct "say it like it is, don't beat around the bush" approach. To that, I say, "No problem." Why? I know that an abundance of business owners love working with a person who is a straight shooter. As a solopreneur, my goal is to find people who want to work with someone who has my personality, and I don't have to serve everyone—I only have to serve the people who want to work with me.

Before I became self-employed, I was constantly told to change my personality. I was told that if I wanted to succeed, I needed to slow down, sugarcoat my words, and not be as truthful with people. That meant, though, pretending to be someone I am not. When I started my business, I was worried that people would not want to work with me because of my behavior. However, I learned that my traits are a big benefit to client attraction. I discovered this in the early days of my business when a new customer who came to me through a referral responded to a comment I made on a phone call when discussing a strategy. They said to me, "I was told I was going to love working with Heather because she's direct and moves super quick!"

While acting out a part and being phony might get you ahead in the corporate world, it doesn't get you anywhere in the small business world. People are attracted to authentic people who are their real selves; fake personalities do not sell. You are the face of your company, and people can see through phoniness. I don't hide who I am. It's the law of attraction—you attract those who like your working style. Be your accurate self, and the universe will lead those to you who will benefit the most from your personality and work ethic. Authenticity is a magnet for a constant stream of dream clients.

Are you worried that something about you will turn people away from doing business with you? Remember what I said about your target market? If you are marketing to everyone, you are marketing to no one. So, tell people about your character. Your target market is composed of people who enjoy working with someone like you. Don't hide who you are, and be proud. Be the powerful person you were born to be. Those who don't like your personality type don't have to do business with you. That's okay. There is a magnitude of people out there to work with.

Peel back the curtain by sharing your stories and photos. If you form a connection with your audience, they will develop trust in you and want to buy from you. Connections can be formed by shared interests and lifestyles. If you have a favorite sports team, have kids, or love a certain type of food, then talk about it, and those with similar interests will love hearing about it.

You might feel vulnerable and afraid of sharing your story and letting others see you; however, the benefits are enormous. Don't let the limiting beliefs, doubts, and insecurities overtake you. Your readers will see how you are courageous for sharing your story and stepping into the arena, and they will admire you for it. If you are transparent, your fans will be impressed with you and see your brilliance and appreciate you as a true, authentic business leader and influencer. If we want to get our message out there, make our mark in the world and create a business that makes a difference, we must be larger than our fears and continually show up.

Prepare your audience for who you are, and they will resonate with you and love you for it.

Consistency

When you are creating a brand, you need to be consistent. It should occur in everything that you do. Brand is your image, and if you are not consistent, it will not have a good impact on the consumers. Consistency will enhance your visibility and enable you to remain in the memory of a consumer.

Make your brand consistent throughout the marketing mix: on business cards, social media, presentations, websites, and more. The fonts, logos, messaging, and colors must always stay the same in your communication tools. By being consistent, your audience will easily remember your company's message—that you are the one to turn to for help and will provide a solution to their dilemma. They will seek you out and want to use your product or services.

So, decide on your fonts, colors, logo, and message, and be consistent on all your materials.

So, What's It Going to Be—Marketing or Branding?

I went in-depth about branding because it's important for your company to have good branding. Put aside a portion of your budget to your branding features, though keep it to a minimum. I have seen people spend a huge amount of their money on their website design, logo, and colors and not have much left for their marketing. To make a bigger difference and to create a fertile business, you need marketing to increase your visibility. Branding alone will never work for your success.

Marketing is what is going to make someone go to your website and contact you for your services. When they visit your website, you want it to look professional and tell visitors the results you provide—that is why you need good branding. But if you don't invest in marketing, no one is ever going to find you, pick up the phone, or type that email to connect with you.

So, establish your branding, give it some thought, and spend some money. However, leave it at that. Focus your time and the largest part of your budget on your marketing. Marketing is the primary way to get business.

Recap

- Branding is about having a professional appearance.
- Branding must be consistent.
- Consistency with your marketing materials will enhance your visibility.
- Brands enhance confidence in a business owner.
- When working on your branding, keep asking WIIFT.
- People buy from a person, not a logo.
- Share your story, and always be authentic.
- Peel back the curtain, and let people see who you are.
- Marketing is the primary way to get business.

Chapter Five

Niche Marketing

We discussed earlier that a small business owner doesn't market to everyone but instead markets only to their target market. A successful entrepreneur has excellent knowledge of their market and uses this in-depth information to effectively connect their message with their audience.

Talking to your audience is done with the marketing mix. Take, for example, the marketing mix component of email marketing. If you are using newsletters to reach potential buyers, you want them written in a way that makes the reader want to open the emails in their inbox, read them, and click the links that lead them to the sales pages to purchase products. Writing effective emails means using the right words that apply to your reader. If your readers are women with families who want a few extra dollars in the bank account and thus are starting a home-based business, you will use words that reach them and will talk about topics that apply to them. If, though, your readers are single women who are looking for dating coaches to help them find romance, you will use different words and talk about different subjects. That's why it's important to get specific and have a good understanding of your audience. Otherwise, you will be sending out emails that get you nowhere.

Next, after you understand your target market, you must further narrow in on them—get more specific. You start with a large group, such as single people (dating coach) or overweight people (weight loss coach). The next step is to drill down on prospects and become more specialized; by becoming more concentrated, you become more sought after because you are more focused and a bigger expert.

There is a saying: "you can't be all things to all people." When you are marketing to everyone, you are marketing to no one. That's why you need to understand the type of people you want to work with and create a niche.

You are now ready for niche marketing.

Example 1: Dating Coach

Let's start with the example of dating coaches. The first thing to do is set up the target market. Instead of being just a general dating coach who helps people of both genders and all ages, the coach decides to be a dating coach for just women or men and to have clients that are a certain age group. In this example, the dating coach concludes to work with just women who are over the age of forty. However, that is not specific enough to attract a clientele.

The coach follows the next step of delving further into their target market. Let's say they know more about divorced career women who are over the age of forty and have a high-level financial status. Instead of being a coach to women with any income level, they create a niche: they decide to be a coach for women who are divorced, are successful in their day jobs, and are between the ages of forty and fifty.

As they are now the influencer in this specific area, the coach will become known more in the singles community and generate more buzz with this specific group of people. Women in their forties will go to them because they are the one who specifically can understand their needs, as opposed to a dating coach who works with anyone. Women who are dating have a different experience than men who are dating, and people in their forties look at things differently than people in their twenties. This coach understands their experiences and talks their language. That is why the women seek this dating coach out—the coach comprehends their mind-set better than other specialists.

Example 2: Public Speaker

Let's say you want to be a public speaker. If you are a speaker, what type of speaking topics do you want to present, what type of audience do you want to attend your forums, and what type of topic and story do you want to share with listeners? Your story needs to fit with the listeners you want to attract to your events. Public speakers range from financial to spiritual to motivational. What age group and gender are the people who should attend, and what industries do they work in? By asking and answering all these questions, you are diving deeper into the market you want to address.

There are numerous events in the industries of finance,

spirituality, and motivation. First, answer which industry you want to speak to, and then select your target listener's gender and age. Dive deeper, and look at their income levels and the field they work in. By getting more focused, you are creating a niche market in the field of speaking.

Let's give the example of an investment speaker for career women. If you are the one who has all the experience with financial seminars for professional women who want to build a nest egg, then when the organizer of a women's gathering is looking for a presenter, they will ask you—that is your niche. Your expertise has helped people invest money. You have taken to the stage for numerous communities and have shared your proficiency with investing. The organizer grasps this by reading your website, media kit, and testimonials from women who write about how you helped them save for the future, and they see photos that show you in front of large crowds of businesswomen. They will pick up the phone and dial your number because you are specialized with the participants who will be attending their next event and have in-depth knowledge of the topic.

If, though, you are a general speaker who gives talks on motivation and financing to both genders and all income levels and ages, you would not be as attractive to the coordinator, and they would not jump at the chance to book you.

Niche marketing is marketing to a specific group of people and a subset of your target market. By choosing a niche, your marketing is simpler and clearer. The group wants to do business with you because you speak their language and understand what they are going through. Your high-level grasp of their needs and problems enables you to effectively use the marketing mix. Your emails, speeches, websites, podcasts, and brochures contain the right language, photos, and slides to communicate.

Having an area of expertise and understanding demographics such as gender, marital status, and income level are all important for creating your niche. To research your niche, you can talk with your current clients and ask them where you excel, and you have the option to pay for research studies, as discussed in an earlier chapter on marketing. A great way to discover your niche is to ask yourself, "Who are the types of people I most enjoy working with, and where do I feel that I add the most value?"

Make sure to look at your own values too. Do you want to work with clients who share your values, goals, and aspirations? Are these your ideal clients? My guess is that you want to align with people who share your morals, so put your values in your equation when determining your niche.

All the components of the marketing mix and your branding match and address the needs of your niche. When creating your branding (logo, tagline, messaging, colors), you will develop it based on your niche.

This book focuses on building your celebrity. I'm going to discuss in a moment how by knowing your niche, you can showcase your expertise to people in your niche when using the marketing mix. However, never discount referrals as a prime way to build your business. That's why it's so important to know your beliefs. If you are working with people who have the same ethics as you, you will continue to attract the people you want to work with. Your clients will refer you to their friends and associates because you are all part of the same value base.

When most people start a business, they set up a general target market; examples are a dating coach, a weight loss coach, or a motivational speaker. That's great, and if you are a new business owner, then I encourage you to take this route and stick with it in the initial setup of your company. Next, after operating their business for a while and increasing their cash flow, entrepreneurs take the new step and hire a coach or a consultant. They are encouraged by their business strategists to become more specialized. However, what usually occurs is the entrepreneur hesitates at setting up a niche as they fear it will turn away potential clients. The truth is, though, the most successful businesses out there have a niche, and they offer a more specific service targeted to a more focused group of people. As a result of being so particular, they attract a huge following and become very profitable.

As a business owner, you need to overcome the fear of becoming more focused and understand the benefits. By having this mind-set, you will form a deeper connection with your prospects, become a client magnet, and be the leader that makes an impact in the world.

Now back to the topic of this book—celebrity marketing. As you understand your niche, you promote yourself to your niche. You can go to networking events where they hang out, speak on radio shows that they listen to, and submit articles to magazines that they read. This will make it much easier to attract your ideal clients and be a superb lead generator. You won't be spending time in places that your niche doesn't frequent, so money and resources will not go to waste.

Recap

- Your niche is a further subset of your target market.
- Understanding your niche lets you effectively use the marketing mix to communicate with your audience.
- To research your niche, talk with clients, and ask them where you excel.
- Discover your niche by asking yourself, "Who are the types of people I most enjoy working with, and where do I add the most value?"
- Your branding and marketing are based on your niche.

Chapter Six

What Is Social Media?

Before I talk about celebrity marketing, I want to take a moment to discuss your social media. My goal is to give you a good understanding of what social media is and is not for small businesses.

Social media is about being social. It's about forming and maintaining a connection with your audience. To create this connection, you share updates with your readers. Updates center around letting followers into the world of the page owner's company: how it functions, what the owner is about, business building tips for success, and so on. They're about the person behind the enterprise name.

When I put together a social media plan for my customers, I discuss with them the recipe needed: insider tips, links to blog posts from their website, posts on industry articles that others have written in leading magazines, promotions for their products, and an overview of their business services. This part of the strategy goes over quite well with people, and they are fine to send me the needed information to set up their social media.

However, when I mention the next parts of the social media recipe—making videos of the owner discussing educational content and posting photos of the owner and their staff in their office and at business functions—I get resistance. A lot of customers just don't want to do it, and it takes a lot of convincing and time for them to get going in these areas.

I understand the hesitation. Many of us are introverts, and we don't want to share everything with strangers. Some of us are afraid of our visual appearance and don't want others to know how we look, and we feel awkward about posting our pictures online. Some customers feel no one will watch a video of them giving a talk, so why bother taking the time to develop one.

However, we must overcome this reluctance and get out there and show ourselves in action. We can't hide. It's the difference between having a mediocre social media presence and a successful one. The people that are out there posting photos and videos of themselves are the ones who shine on social media.

If you don't want to share personal photos of yourself online, that's okay. There is no need to share family images with your spouse and children or your house. What I'm saying is share pictures of your business life: snapshots of you on stage when you do public speaking, as an exhibitor at an event, or with your customers from your last meeting in your office.

Why share these videos and photos? The answer is simply because it's the proof of your success. It lets people learn about you and see who you are.

People are very visual, and they are going to remember a photo more than anything you have written on your page. You need images to stay on top of people's minds and to reinforce what you are saying.

If you are claiming to be an influencer in your field, you need to show it to your social media fans. If you are a coach who helps people with public speaking, then show an image of you on stage speaking, along with a note beside the image that explains the location of where you delivered the presentation. For example, "Had a great time last night speaking to the ladies of X. It was an amazing turnout. The room was packed and full of amazing energy." If you are a real estate agent who helps people find their dream homes, then show pictures of you with happy customers after the sale is complete with a sign that says, "SOLD." Include a note with the post that explains the picture. "Congrats to X on your new home!" If you are a yoga instructor, then show a snapshot of you teaching a class to a roomful of participants and put a note that talks about the yoga position you are teaching in the photo.

Photos add credibility and proof that you are who you say you are. They don't have to be just you doing your work but can show behind-the-scenes actions. Here are some examples: a photo of you at your desk with the caption "At my desk before I get ready to get on the phone for a 9 a.m. call with a client"; a picture with an associate at a networking event with the caption "With X at Y event last night"; or a snapshot of you at the exhibitor booth with the caption "Setting up my booth for X event last night. So many friendly people stopped by to talk and ask about my services. It was a great success!"

All these photos let people see that you are busy, have

clients, and are a successful person. They let people learn about you and make them want to say yes to working with you.

Videos that you post on your pages let people see you in action. They can be video lessons, podcasts, or just you on your way to a business function. Videos are the same as photos: they let the audience know about you and further demonstrate your leadership in the industry.

Combining photos and videos with the rest of what you are doing on your social media pages makes a huge impact. The readers grasp that you are who you say you are and will be driven to further connect with you—leading to future sales down the road.

You need the complete mix, though. Photos and videos online are not enough, and blog posts and tips alone are for sure not enough. A social media plan should include a good mix where every day you post something different.

I'll tell it to you straight right now: if you are not sharing photos of you, your social media pages will not go anywhere. While I'm sharing with you in this book many examples of my clients' success online, I'm going to peel back my own curtain now and tell you of a failure that I had with a client.

The client was an author and had just published a book. I read a portion of the book and her blog posts. She wrote about self-knowledge, spirituality, and how to achieve inner peace. The client was a great writer, and I loved her content because it was authentic. However, I could not get her to share a photo of herself on her website and social media pages; she did not want any picture of herself to be online. The profile picture on all her pages was a logo. I put together valuable tips on her topics and was able to grow her followers somewhat. People who visited her social media pages did like the content and would write so in the comments. However, the analytical data revealed that no one was clicking the links to her blog, and she had no book sales achieved with social media. I spent a long time trying to get her to put a picture at least in her profile image. She wouldn't do so, and eventually, without any sales coming in, she no longer needed my services.

From this situation, I cracked the code that social media was more than just content and that it's about the person behind the page. It's about audiences wanting to connect with the writer of the content and not just the content itself. From that point on, I made it a point to never work with someone who would not show their face. I even added to that requirement that they must agree to create videos to post online. If potential clients do not want to post pictures of themselves or create videos, then I don't work with them; I know the pages will not harvest any rewards, and the only result will be deadwood. For the social media garden to bloom, you need a mix of photos, videos, and content.

The clients that I now work with always use the combination of articles, blog posts, tips, videos, and photos of their faces. As a result of using the complete recipe, my clients achieve incredible results: their audience clicks the links to read their blog posts and sign up for their giveaways. My clients form connections with their online fans and gradually see an increase of sales.

Your Online Portfolio

One of the biggest misconceptions about social media is that it is a way to get customers. People see your social media pages, are impressed with what you are saying, and will go right away to buy from you. This can't be further from the truth.

Social media has different goals, and if you use each goal properly, you will get customers.

The first goal: social media's purpose is to maintain connections. If you are following the tools that I have outlined throughout this book, then you are a business owner going to networking events and doing speaking engagements. Now that someone has heard you speak or has your business card in hand from a networking function, you want them to remember you. They might not need your services right away, but they might need them in the future. If you made a great speech, they might remember you in six months to call you, but how are they going to find you? Most likely they did not save the link with the web page of your information, and they also are not going to dig through that pile of business cards buried somewhere in their office. However, if you connect on social media with attendees following each event you attend, then when they need your services, they will be easily able to find you. Because your posts will be appearing regularly in their newsfeed, you will be top of mind. You have maintained the newly formed connection, and they can now find you and hire you.

The second goal of social media is that it serves as a portfolio and an "About" page of your website, a place for people to go check you out. If someone is impressed with your elevator speech or your speech from the stage that they heard at an event, they are most likely not just going to hire you. They will first check you out in detail. They will go to your website and then your social media. If your website looks great with branding and professionalism and is easy to navigate, they will be impressed. This will add to their initial impression of you from the meeting where they were first introduced to you. Next, they will go to your social media, and if they see a page filled with great information and photos, that will further enhance their image of you.

I once heard from a strategist's training seminar that your website does not need a blog; people don't read a website's articles, and thus you don't need to bother with having a blog. While it is true that most people are not going to sit there reading your blog for hours, what they will do is glance at it, and if they see some great titles, they will be impressed. They will choose a few blog posts and skim through them, and if you are writing great and relevant information, your blog will add to their impression of you, and they will want to hire you.

The same goes with your social media. Put out on your social media pages your blog posts with images and the links back to your website. As someone checks you out, they will see that you have written all these blog posts on this topic, and they will understand that you are an expert. They will click on a few links to read more. The purpose of the links is for potential clients to learn about your knowledge in your industry.

It doesn't matter if loads of people visit your site and social media pages and click the links; what does matter is that the people who truly want to hire you like what they see when they visit.

Clients use different approaches when researching a person they are considering hiring: some will spend more time surfing your website, and some will spend more time on your social media pages. Some prospects will pay more attention to your videos or giveaways. Some will look at everything in detail, while others will skim the information. The point is that each person has a different method. Thus, for each area where you are demonstrating your talents, make sure it is done well, and don't ignore an area and let it look poor.

That is how to treat your website, social media pages, blog, and podcast—as a portfolio of your work. Instead of bringing in a huge laminated display to showcase who you are, you showcase your talents through these different systems. Instead of pointing people to these platforms to learn about you, they are going to each one on their own.

A prospective client might not call you today, but they might call you in a few months. You are planting the seed for them to have an interest in learning more about you. When you set up the right roots in your garden, it flourishes in the future.

You planted the seed at a speaking event or with your giveaway or when you made a guest appearance on a radio show, and now you are keeping in touch with the audience. They will research you and contact you when they need you.

If, though, you had a great speech and gave out your business card and your audience encountered a poorly designed site, poorly written blog, or poorly set up social media pages, they will have no interest in working with you.

Social media is not about someone seeing a few amazing posts and then picking up the phone to hire you. Someone is not going to read one blog on your website and call you or see a website with great branding and then reach out to you. It's about connecting with people through public speaking, networking, and giveaways and then maintaining the connection by posting on social media on a regular basis. Combining everything is what is going to make you the star that gets people to pull out their wallets.

Recap

- Social media is about being social.
- You must share videos and pictures of yourself on social media pages.
- People are visual and will remember a photo more than written content.
- The first goal of social media is to maintain connections.
- The second goal of social media is that it serves as a portfolio and "About" page for prospective clients to learn about you.

Chapter Seven

Traditional Marketing vs. Celebrity Marketing

Traditional marketing involves going to people and informing them about your offer and the value of working with you or using your product, which is then followed by asking for the sale.

Traditional marketing is educating the audience with free content, articles, e-books, and social media posts. Educational content can include business tips, success quotes, how-to suggestions, ways to make improvements, and more.

The traditional model uses advertising, cold calls, emails, websites, and blogs. If you are a service-based business, you would highlight on materials and phone calls the benefits of working with your team: knowledge, prompt response time, excellent support, number of years in business, and so on.

On the other hand, celebrity marketing means you impress people by letting them know about your success. Your audience sees you online and is fascinated with what you are all about, and they want to work with you. You get in front of people by speaking and writing books and articles, and afterward you tell everyone all about the experience. You increase your visibility.

The main goal of celebrity marketing is to attract clients, not chase them. You attract clients by showcasing expertise in a field; customers want to work with you because you are well-known and an influencer in your industry.

To understand celebrity marketing, we must look at the word celebrity. What does celebrity mean? It means "celebrate." We think of the word celebrity in terms of movie stars and famous people, but let us look at the word in the context of someone being renowned for what they do. Hollywood people are famous for making movies, and we are celebrating their success and fame because they are film stars. As an entrepreneur, do the same thing with your marketing, and celebrate your successes of being on podcasts or speaking at summits by letting everyone in your marketing channels know.

Being a celebrity doesn't mean everybody in the whole world knows about you. You need to be a celebrity in your niche. Think of people who are well known to just people who follow their industry, such as the gurus and CEOs of companies who specialize in specific markets. These gurus are not known to people who don't follow their industry. JJ Virgin is a famous nutrition expert for people who are focused on health, Tony Robbins is a motivational speaker for audiences that want self-improvement assistance, and

Ali Brown is a coach for women entrepreneurs. Not everybody has heard of them, and people who are not interested in the services they offer will most likely never hear of them. However, the people who are attracted to their areas of specialty might at some point hear of them and follow them. Why? They are all leaders in their fields.

That's your goal. You want to be known in your niche. You want to go to speaking events, appear on podcasts, and write for magazines that the members of your niche attend and read; that's how the buzz about you will be created. That's why niche marketing is so important to understand and accomplish.

You need to create your celebrity to grow your business. Celebrity is built by showcasing your published articles and speaking engagements. The place to display your celebrity is in the marketing mix of emails, social media, blogs, and so on. If you position yourself as an expert in these channels, people will become excited to follow and listen to you.

As a business owner who is using celebrity marketing, you will also be using traditional marketing; it's not just use one and abandon the other. You are still going to be telling your audience about how great your products and services are. But you are also increasing your visibility and letting followers learn about all your speaking engagements and published articles. The idea is that they learn about all your public appearances, and as they are impressed, they then consider hiring you for your services. They take your company more seriously and have more of an interest in learning about you because you are an influencer in your field.

As you use celebrity marketing, readers are more likely to open the next email you send them instead of just deleting it, and they will go to your website to learn about your business. When you call them on the phone, they will not just hang up but instead want to have a conversation with you. You have stood out in the crowd from a list of people who offer the same products and services. Celebrity marketing has made you unique.

Share Your Success

Being a success in today's business world means you must show off. Many of us are discouraged from showing off our accomplishments. Parents, teachers, and friends suggest that it's not nice to rub our success onto other people and that no one likes a show-off. Another reason that many people do not want to share their success is that they feel it invades others' private space.

Let me tell it to you straight—you must show off. You should be proud of your accomplishments and let others know about them. You don't get anywhere in the online world without telling everybody about your triumphs. You need to toot your own horn.

Consider a job interview. When you go into a job interview, you tell the interviewer about your achievements at your previous places of employment. If you are applying for a position in sales, you are going to let the hiring person know about the awards you have won, the quotas you met, the raving customers you worked with, and the excellent job evaluations you received. You know you need to mention all these accomplishments so you can get the job, and if you don't mention your feats, the interviewer won't be impressed, and they won't hire you.

It's the same thing now that you are self-employed. If you want a prospect to hire you, you must let them know how great you are. You will share with them customer testimonials and portfolios (traditional marketing) and inform them of the podcasts you have spoken on and magazines where your articles have appeared (celebrity marketing). You want them to know about your achievements the same way you want the job interviewer to know. By sharing with potential clients your success stories, you will impress them, and they will want to work with you.

When someone meets you at a networking event or receives a referral from someone to use your services, they are going to check you out before they book an appointment. They will go to your website, skim through it, and take a quick look at your social media channels; you want to wow them. If they see a bunch of blog posts where you are writing about your niche, videos of you speaking on YouTube, and posts about speaking engagements on Facebook and Instagram, think of how awestruck they will be.

Showcase Your Celebrity

As I mentioned in an earlier chapter, people buy from a person and not a logo. Your audience wants to know about the person writing the newsletters, blog posts, and social media content, and thus it is instrumental that you are out there online showing your face and telling your stories. Your followers want to see a real living person before they hand over a credit card number.

I discussed how marketing means getting out there. It means writing articles, doing speaking engagements, and more. Doing all these things establishes you as a specialist in your field, and you will become a sought-after expert in your niche.

I've worked with clients who have invited guests onto

their podcasts and radio shows, and many times these guests do not discuss with their own audience that they spoke on my client's podcast. They don't invite the audience to listen to what they had to say on the show. To tell you straight, it amazes me that they don't share it! Think about it. You are a guest on an online program. Why don't you share it with everyone? If you are invited to speak, wouldn't you want to let everyone know? Wouldn't you want to impress people? If they hear you are on a program, maybe they will be so impressed that they will purchase your services. Don't you want your online community to go watch the show you were on? Perhaps they will be motivated by what you had to say and will want to work with you.

I'm sad to say that many people don't share their public collaborations. They miss out! Not sharing their ventures is what makes them a business that is just getting by as opposed to a business that is impacting the world and making massive amounts of money.

The customers that I work with who share with their networks their speaking events are the ones who prosper. They are the ones who are doing effective marketing, are generating six to seven figures with their businesses, are perceived as influencers in their field, and are client magnet machines.

Many times, when you appear on a telesummit or a podcast, you are required to share it to your marketing channels. However, don't just share it because it's part of the agreement with you and the organization. Even if they don't request it, share it anyway! Celebrate, and let everyone know!

A great reason to share your speaking appearances is to give thanks to the person who let you appear as a guest on their program. If they took the time to have you on their show, did not charge you, and let you promote your content to their audience, why are you not saying thank you? If they are helping you grow your audience, then you should help them grow their audience by sharing the show with your network. You need to reciprocate.

In addition, consider the long-term benefits of reciprocating. If a year after the show is broadcast the show needs another guest, perhaps they will think of you and invite you to make another appearance. After all, they know they can count on you because you went out and did your part by promoting your appearance. However, if you didn't publicize it, why should they have you back on?

You might not be invited to be a guest on their show again, but maybe you will be invited to be a presenter at another event they are organizing, such as a telesummit or a live public gig. With so many possibilities out there, don't dismiss the importance of co-promotion and doing your part.

When you co-promote on social media, make sure to always share the link and tag the hosts on all posts. Pretty much every social network allows for a tag option. Using the tagging feature will let the host know that you are mentioning them, and they will be grateful for your actions. Most likely when they see the mention, they will share your post also to their networks, giving you additional exposure. You should also forward them a copy of any email that you send out to your list that mentions your guest appearance.

There are many ways to celebrate your speaking success. Post on social media that you gave a talk somewhere, but also include a photo. If you appeared on a podcast, the photo should contain your picture and the logo of the organization, or your picture and the host's picture or all three—your picture, the host's picture, and the logo for the podcast. If your speaking success was for a live event, such as a networking chapter, post an image of you on the stage at the event with text that says, "I loved speaking at X chapter yesterday. My topic was Y." You can also have someone take a three-minute video segment of your speech and then upload it. These types of pictures and videos provide proof that you spoke and show that you can get in front of an audience. Remember, people are very visual.

The same thing is true when writing blog posts. If you're writing about something that you are an expert at, show a photo in the blog posts that features you in action. For example, if you are discussing on your blog how to be a great speaker because you are a speaking coach, then post a photo of you on stage at an event; this will enhance the point you are talking about in the article. If you are providing weight loss tips in your blog post because you are a weight loss coach, then show before and after images of a client. People will read the article and see the photos of your customer, which further provide proof that you are a leader and expert in your field and that you have clients who hire you. Make sure to share these articles to your social media pages along with the snapshots.

Perhaps someone came up to you after an event and told you they loved your talk. Ask them for their name and permission to use their compliment. Post in your channels a graphic of their testimonial with their name and the title and date of the speaking gig that the testimonial refers to. By sharing this graphic with your audience, you show how great a success you are.

Celebrity marketing is a process and takes hard work and time. As you grow your celebrity, you will get a constant stream and steady flow of new clients, and you will raise your rates. As your name and attraction grow, more followers will seek you out on social media, and you will be more in demand with people wanting to work with you. It's a chain effect. However, you must remember it takes time and does not happen overnight. The best approach is to choose a few areas of the marketing mix to focus on and excel at them.

Recap

- Traditional marketing involves going to people and informing them about your offer.
- Traditional marketing is sharing educational content.
- Celebrity marketing is impressing people by letting them know about your success to increase your visibility.
- Celebrity marketing uses public speaking, podcast hosting, making appearances, and article writing.
- Celebrity marketing focuses on being a celebrity in your niche.
- You need to showcase your celebrity to be a success.

Chapter Eight

What Is Public Speaking?

I want to take some time now to talk about the necessity of speaking. I have worked with clients who don't do any speaking and focus their time just on having giveaways, sending out newsletters, and posting on social media. I have also worked with clients who spend their time on the giveaways, emails, and social media but also spend their time on the components of the speaking mix. The customers who don't do any speaking don't have as much success as the ones who do speak, and they don't get a steady flow of people who want to work with them. I now make it a requirement that to work with me, clients must want to take part in public speaking. If they don't want to do speaking to grow their business, I will not sign on to do their marketing because I know I will not be able to achieve for them business growth results.

Speaking is what adds to your success as an entrepreneur and makes people say yes to working with you. Many people think that the way to success is sitting behind a computer, blogging, and writing on social media. This can't be further from the truth. Sitting behind a computer is not enough. You need to get out there and deliver heartfelt talks if you want to generate buzz for your business and be a client magnet machine.

The fastest way to cash is public speaking. I've heard people say this expression many times, and let me tell you, it is very true.

Think about it for a minute.

At an event where most attendees are the target audience, the goal is for the seller to get as many people in attendance to seek out their services. A presenter at the front of the room got there because the event organizer knows they are an expert in their field and can deliver a great keynote talk. The organizer has agreed to let them speak because the presenter is a leader, and the audience understands their leadership before the presenter even commences the speech. Once they have given a great presentation that demonstrates their abundance of knowledge, they will make a big impression, and people will want to work with them. Speaking is a great way to promote your company.

There are many places to speak online and off-line (Facebook Live, podcasts, webinars, live networking functions, etc.), and I will discuss these options in the next chapters. Speaking online and off-line gives you credibility and authority. You are at the front of the room—at the podium and not in a crowd of people. You stand out. People take notice and proceed to talk to you after your speech. You have positioned yourself as the leader, and the audience will follow you.

Another mistaken assumption is that to be a successful speaker, you must give an entertaining talk that is theatrical and full of humor. However, public speaking for business must be from a place of education and expertise, and the most successful speeches are not ones that entertain but ones that engage. It is not hard to make a great speech; it needs to be structured, well rehearsed, thought out, educational, and full of valuable content. If it contains all these features, you are set.

Remember the rule that you are always answering WIIFT—What's in it for them? The speech is not about you and your experience, education, services, and such—it's about what the audience needs. Choose a topic you know your audience is struggling with, and show them the solution. The best way to begin a speech is to delve right away into the topic and give your bio and services at the end. Educational content is 80 percent of what you deliver, and your bio and offer are 20 percent.

A great speech needs to have four things:
- Great content.
- A way to capture the audience's attention that makes them want to learn more about you and work with you.
- A way to convert the audience to your offer.
- A way for listeners to connect with you for the next steps.

The content of your speech should be educational. You are selling to your audience without being salesy. Decide on a topic that is related to your services where you have expertise. For example, if you are a weight loss coach, give a talk on five tips to lose weight after the holidays. Your talk will be informative and provide great information. Although you will not give away your whole strategy and approach that people pay you for, it is still going to be a discussion of superb content. Though the rest of the supersecret techniques for weight loss are not shared, the weight loss coach does give five amazing tools to lose weight that do indeed work.

The audience will be impressed with your talk if you capture their attention by giving a hot title and fabulous information. They will be interested in learning more about you because you have captured their interest by approaching the discussion from a place of education and not selling.

Toward the end of the presentation, provide the offer. For example, it can be to book a free thirty-minute introductory session, or it can be a special discount for your next paid event. Always make sure to link your offer to your speech. You could say, "I know many people are struggling with this, and I hope today I have provided you with actionable steps to implement that you can use right away. If you would like further guidance on this topic, I have five slots available in my calendar for a free thirty-minute session. These openings are available to the first five people who sign up."

Because you gave a great speech from a place of education and expertise, it is now easy to make a sale, and attendees will want to book a session with you or be present for your next paid event. If attendees do not purchase from you or sign up for the session, many of them will still be impressed and want to stay in touch; they will go ahead and proceed to follow you online and join your email list (remember, planting seeds).

Recap

- Public speaking gives you credibility and authority.
- There are many places to speak online and off-line (Facebook Live, podcasts, webinars, live networking functions, etc.).
- People pay more attention to public speakers and are more likely to talk to the speaker after the speech.
- You need to do more than sit behind a computer, blog, and talk on social media.
- Presentations are always answering WIIFT— What's in it for them?
- Educational content is 80 percent of what you deliver, and the bio and offer are 20 percent.
- Toward the end of the presentation, provide the offer.

Chapter Nine

Where to Speak Online

In the upcoming sections, I'm going to discuss the different avenues to take for getting in front of an online audience to promote your business. However, you don't have to use everyone that I'm going to talk about; my suggestion is to find two or three that work for you and dive into them. Let's say one of the ones you select is being a guest on a podcast—that means speaking on podcasts two to three times a month and not one podcast every six months. The more podcasts you speak on, the better, and if it is working for you, then be a guest as often as possible on podcasts. Remember, though, it is not enough to just be a guest; you need to share your appearances on social media, blog posts, and newsletters.

The Speaking Online Mix

- Hosting podcasts
- Being a guest on podcasts and radio shows
- Hosting video shows on Facebook and YouTube
- Creating Your Own Facebook Group
- Being a Guest on Telesummits
- Hosting and co-hosting webinars
- Having television spots on news shows

Hosting Your Own Podcast

Hosting a podcast is a great way to be a celebrity. Having your own show where you share your business strategies with an audience on a regular basis will enhance your credibility to your listeners, and they will see you as an expert. They will tune in regularly to hear what you have to say on the latest topics revolving around your niche. By seeing you discuss your expertise as well as reading the comments and reviews of your show, people will see your status as a leader in your field.

Your podcast will address topics that are relevant to your niche target audience, and as your target market wants to learn this information, they will tune in because it's important to them. Making sure you attract the right listeners to your podcast is another important reason to research your target market.

With your podcast, make sure to put the podcast show on your website, social media pages, and newsletter. Don't expect people to find out about your show on their own. You must get out there, tell your followers about the show, and give them the links. You should have the show embedded on your website so that when they visit your website, they will easily be able to hit the play button and listen.

By reading about the podcast on social media, emails, and websites, your followers will learn that you are a host of a show and know that you are an influencer in your field. When they listen in, the podcast will further enhance their opinion of you.

A great way to further enhance that you are a leader in your field and promote your name is to bring on guests for your show. Your credibility will be enhanced when listeners hear that other names in the industry are appearing on your podcast, and you will look like a true influencer. This superstar status will lead to brand new high-paying clients seeking you out.

Make it a requirement that guests must co-promote their appearance of their episode on their social media channels and emails as well. By making this mandatory, you will gain a larger audience of listeners because people who have never heard of you will now learn about you. Because the businessperson they respect was on your program as a guest, they will now consider you a leading authority as well. After all, the highly respected leader they follow would go on a program run only by an authority in their niche. New listeners of this episode will tune into future episodes, will want to follow you on social media, and will also consider working with you.

Promote your programs that have guests, and the bigger the name, the more you need to promote it. Think of the buzz that you will generate if you have this big name in your industry on your show.

Have great graphics for your podcast. Each episode should have a nice graphic with the episode number, and when you have a guest, put the guest's name in the graphic.

This way, when someone checks you out online, they will see all the visual images of the invitees you have had and will be impressed. Even if they don't know all the guests, think of the positive impression they will have when they see many names—you must be someone important who was able to book all those people! By following these steps, you are truly using celebrity marketing.

Once your podcast is live and several episodes are aired, put in your bio that you are the host of your own show. Your website bio, your speaker bio, and your social media bio should all mention the podcast, and as people discover that you have your own program, they will begin to consider you a prestigious business leader.

Do you want to book more speaking events? Do you want to be a guest on other radio shows? Think of the leverage that your podcast will give you! As you request to be on other shows, let the hosts know you have a show as well, and they will want to have you on their program because they can then ask to be a guest on one of your episodes. You will get more amazing people for your show and more speaking engagements just for hosting a podcast.

If you are considering at this moment about having a podcast, you are probably asking yourself how often you need to create an episode. Daily, weekly, biweekly, monthly? First, I will respond by saying you don't need to do it daily. The best I would say is weekly or every two weeks, and make it a point to stick to the amount you decide. While you don't have to get the episode out at the same time each week (for example, every Tuesday at 9 a.m.), you should still be consistent with your release times. If someone goes to your iTunes and YouTube pages and sees a sporadic number of episodes—sometimes weekly, then monthly, and then a break for a few months, and then back to every two weeks—

it won't give them confidence in your show, and they won't subscribe. If, though, they see that the show airs on a regular basis, they will believe in you and will sign up.

So, choose a promotion schedule and strategy, and stick to them. Decide what you want to do for each new episode. Will you send out a solo email or just put a mention in your newsletter? Or will you do both? Will you have one post or several posts on social media? The main thing is to get the word out. Just don't be inconsistent where for one episode you have lots of social media content and then for other episodes no content—it just doesn't give a good impression. Do the same amount of promotion for each show, and if you have a famous guest, then for that appearance, increase the promotion a bit more than usual.

Take snapshots of the reviews that appear on iTunes, Stitcher, your website, and your social media pages; share them in your emails and social media pages; and put a screenshot of a great review as a solo post. The goal is to impress people with how well you are doing by letting them know what a listener thought and that they too can listen in to the program. Remember, if you want to drive massive sales, you must toot your horn. You are a star, and by showcasing your celebrity to your followers, they will learn about and be impressed by you, will see you as an influencer, and will want to work with you.

Podcasts started out with primarily iTunes, Stitcher, and Podbean; however, now you can post your podcast on YouTube and Facebook. Record each episode with video and audio, send the audio file to the podcast hosting companies, upload the video to both Facebook and YouTube, and share the links on Twitter and LinkedIn. For the audio file, don't put the episode on just one service, like iTunes, but put it out on as many channels as possible. The more places the program appears and the more ways people can watch and listen to your show, the more people you will have listening to your show, and the better it is for you.

Podcasts take a lot of time to produce, and you must focus on them extensively. Don't start a podcast, do a few episodes, and give up. Most likely your podcast will not have a lot of listeners at the beginning, but they will pick up over time. Your podcast is a garden, and it takes a lot of watering and plowing before it becomes fertile, the seeds begin to grow, and the plants begin to blossom.

I have been coordinating a client's podcast for over four years. Today it is a leading podcast that has a huge number of listeners; however, her podcast did not sprout until after one year. My client did not give up with low listeners; instead, she kept working on her podcast because she understood that in time the podcast would bear fruit. We would meet and discuss strategies to grow the audience. The solutions we put in place to increase listeners were advertising, more social media mentions, and more emails about the show. We also now mention older episodes on social media; the episodes were evergreen and thus are still relevant. By focusing and continually applying these strategies, the listeners flourished over time.

Being a Guest on Podcasts and Radio Shows

We have just covered the benefits of having your own podcast—now let's talk about the benefits of being a guest on podcasts.

Being a guest on a podcast is a great way to promote your company. You will get in front of the host's listeners, who will learn about you and your specialty. Most podcasts enable the guest to discuss a bit about their services and promote their giveaways. Usually you will gain new social media followers and visits to your website because of your guest appearance. Being a podcast guest is a great way to increase your celebrity.

Once you have spoken, make sure to ask the host for the air date, and when you know the air date, promote your appearance. As I discuss elsewhere in this book, many times someone is a guest and doesn't share the episode with their followers. They are missing out on a great opportunity! Think about how impressed your audience will be when they find out that you were invited to speak on a show. It shows that you are a sought-after speaker, that someone thinks you have valuable content to discuss, and that you are someone of importance. You are a celebrity. You are the real deal, and being a guest is a great way to catapult your business forward.

However, many people instead choose not to promote their guest appearances. How are people going to find out and set aside the time to listen in? How are you going to grow your business without letting others know?

Promote the show you were a guest on by posting the show on social media, writing a blog post that has the embedded episode in it, and mentioning it along with the link in an email to your list. Make sure on social media to tag the host and say thank you; this way, they will be thankful that you are promoting the show and will more likely remember you in the future for other opportunities. There are so many different types of joint venture opportunities out there—attending telesummits, coauthoring books, speaking at events, and so on. Most likely, if someone is hosting a podcast, they are involved in a lot of other projects.

On your website, create a page on speaking. The page should include the places you have spoken in person and online, and for the online places, include the links to the podcasts where you were a guest. As someone checks out your website, they will see the places you have spoken and will be impressed.

Usually a podcast is evergreen, so while you for sure should promote the episode the most during the air date, it doesn't mean it ends there. Remind your audience of your appearance later. Every four months or so, make a mention of it, and give the link. People will be captivated whether it's in the present or the past. Even if readers saw the link the first time you posted it, there is so much content online that they will not remember it four months in the future. New people who are now following you did not read your older content, and that is another good reason to keep repeating your guest appearances.

Some podcasts are more prestigious and have larger audiences than others because the hosts are more established and famous. However, don't discount the smaller ones. I have had customers who got clients and larger followings on social media by also appearing on the not-so-well-known programs. A small audience still means someone is listening. When you post your guest appearances on social media, the readers aren't going to say that the unknown podcasts are not striking; rather, they will be impressed that you got speaking engagements. Although a famous program will capture their attention more, they will still be affected by the not-so-famous ones. So, share all shows you appear on, and don't discriminate.

Hosting Video Shows on Facebook and YouTube

Don't wait for others to have you on their shows. Host your own. The benefits of videos are similar to podcasts, and

---

the process of setting up podcasts is very similar to setting up a video series. Podcasts are uploaded to sites such as iTunes, Stitcher, and Podbean, while video shows are streamed on Facebook and YouTube.

Facebook and YouTube videos can be done live or can be pre-recorded and uploaded; both have their benefits.

Pre-recorded means that you can edit the video, so if you make a mistake, it's easy to fix. You can't fix live videos—so make sure you rehearse and are prepared before you hit the button to go live. The main benefits of hosting a Facebook Live or YouTube Live are that you can interact with the audience, and they can post questions in the comments that you can reply to on the spot. Going live online makes watchers feel part of your community.

With live video, make sure to invite people to your event ahead of time. There's no point in having a great topic but not publicizing it before you go on air. If no one knows about the livestream, no one will be present. Let people know by sending out an email, mentioning it on your social media channels, creating a Facebook event, and posting the dates on the home page of your website.

When you are live streaming, encourage questions. Tell your attendees to post their questions in the comments section and that you will answer as many as you can. Inform viewers to introduce themselves, and say hi to each person as they log on for the show. By following these strategies and encouraging participation, you will be creating a fun learning environment that has a welcoming spirit. Your video show will make people look forward to your future shows, and the next time the show occurs, people will set aside time to tune in.

If you are setting up a livestream, by watching you interact with your audience, the viewers discover a warm, friendly, and professional person who cares about others. The qualities are demonstrated in live video sessions as you encourage questions and then patiently answer them. Thus, make sure to always encourage questions. (Questions can be posted in the chat box of a livestream or the comments section of your Facebook group or page.) Always show that you are grateful for the questions asked by mentioning the questioner's name and thanking them for the question.

The benefits of videos are that people see your face, learn about you, and get a feel for who you are and what it's like to work with you. As you answer questions and share information on an important topic, they see that you are a leader—you are now more recognized in the industry. Think of how impressed they will be when you answer their questions! An audience member needed clarification on something, and you are the one who provided the solution! The other audience members will be spellbound that you were able to answer this question live without any preparation. A further wow for participants is that you are hosting such an event and getting people to turn out. Only an icon can accomplish such a feat.

Videos are not just there for you to show your audience that you are a leader in your industry. They also enable the audience to see other facets of you, such as your working style and personality. Videos focused on showcasing your personality enable you to gain more fans, and thus they also build your celebrity.

Whether the video is pre-recorded or live, the viewer will see who you are as a person by watching the video. In the videos, introduce yourself and your business, teach a lesson, and give stories from your life and your clients' lives as examples to back up the lesson. Talk slowly, have a smile on your face, and show your passion and belief with your topic when talking.

Videos are great when introducing a product to your audience. As you introduce your new program to your followers, create a video that discusses the opportunity. Talk about the benefits of your new offer and answer questions. Your warmth and enthusiasm will connect more with the audience than just an email and a sales page and will be an effective tool to drive orders and boost profits.

Another thing you can do with video is invite other business experts to be a guest on your video program. Inform your list about this guest, and make sure your guest shares it with their list. If you were able to have this person book time with you, it demonstrates that you are someone of importance and knowledge. Telling everyone about your prestige is a way to cement your celebrity status to your niche. Go for it!

Repetition with video is of key importance. Don't just do a great job with your video, air it once, and move on to something else. You did a great job, so show it off to your community. Share the recording: post the link on all your social media channels, do a video blog (vlog) about it, and send out an email to your list. If the live recording was on Facebook, post it on YouTube, and post it again on Facebook at a future date. Let your followers know that you created a video of great content that is free and that they should go and watch it to learn something. Many times people do a video once and then forget it—a poor strategy. You need to share the video many, many, many times.

The first time you share the recording (the day after it airs), your post could be in this format: "Did you miss my Facebook Live on topic X yesterday? It was great. We had loads of great questions, such as . . . If you missed the video, no worries. Just click here to watch the recording." Share the recording again the following week with a reminder of what you did last week. Then share it again every two months. You made a great video. Don't hide it from people; let as many out there know about it as possible. By following this process, you will watch your online visibility soar with unlimited potential, and the more the world gets to see your magical gifts, the more you become a leading marketing machine.

Creating Your Own Facebook Group

In addition to the traditional Facebook page that most businesses out there have, an additional tactic on Facebook is the Facebook group. Create a group around a topic that you are an expert in, and encourage members to post to the group using the methods that work for them to achieve success. For example, if you are a weight loss coach, create a free group on healthy living, and encourage members to share their approaches on how healthy living made a difference for them and helped them lose weight.

Being the leader of the group gets you to the front of the crowd. You are the one setting the rules for members, encouraging posts, and always replying to comments. The group description lists you as the founder. The description section can also include your bio—which is another benefit, as participants will get to learn about you.

Another important thing that you will do is post videos and do Facebook Lives right there in the group. Your videos will answer member questions and concerns and provide insights on how members can overcome their challenges. Saying hi to members as they log on to your Facebook Live and replying to questions during the streaming will show how you are interested in truly helping the others.

Being the leader of a Facebook group lets members get to know you and learn about you and your business. You become a celebrity to the members because you stand out from the crowd and are someone of importance whom they look up to. Just make sure to not create a free group and never participate. Success with a Facebook group all depends on how you show up.

Make sure to take advantage of being the group champion. You can post about your paid programs and offers and mention them in your videos. However, don't get overly promotional; follow the 80-20 rule (80 percent free educational content and 20 percent sales content). Sales will chime in as the members become familiar with you and begin to see the great results that you can deliver.

Being a Guest on Telesummits

Telesummits are online events that feature many guest speakers (usually around five to twenty). Usually someone will host a telesummit based on a topic and then invite experts on this topic to participate. Each expert will do an interview with the host or do their own presentation on the topic, and at the end of the interview or presentation, the guest announces giveaways or pay-for offers.

Telesummits are a great way to grow your email list and social media following. When you are a guest, provide a superb giveaway so the listeners go and sign up for your newsletter. Your presentation and interview need to be stellar so the attendees of the telesummit want to follow you on social media.

Presenting on a virtual conference puts you in the limelight. Listeners know that you are an industry luminary because that is why the host selected you.

Here are some suggestions on how to get invited to take part in virtual conferences. If you are a member of a mastermind group, let the others in the group know you would be interested in taking part in a telesummit if any of them are planning on hosting one. Post in Facebook groups that you would be interested in being invited to any summits. If you host a podcast or video program, then some of the guests you have invited will at some point return the favor and invite you to be interviewed for their online event.

If someone has asked you to be a guest on their online event, they are for sure going to require you to publicize it. The organizer is advertising the summit and promoting your appearance and is most likely not charging you for your attendance, or they are charging you only a small fee. Putting together a telesummit is a lot of work for the planner—show your appreciation and create marketing campaigns for the event. As discussed with podcasts, speaking, and video shows, you will want to publicize that you are a guest on the telesummit because it demonstrates to your fan base that you are a leader, enables more of your followers to learn about you, and adds to your online celebrity status.

If you do your part and market the telesummit, the planner will be happy that they made the right choice by inviting you. If they have future collaborations that they invite others to down the road, they will most likely think of someone who promoted a prior event than someone who did not.

I have assisted with the organization and management of several telesummits, and I know they are a lot of hard work. For the ones I assisted with, participants were all required to sign a contract that they would market the event. Part of my job was to track if participants were promoting the event by asking for social media snapshots and the emails that went out to their lists. Although most people complied and were more than happy to do their part, there were always at least two people for each summit whom I had to remind several times to do the marketing. My emails and phone calls got ignored by these participants, and the organizer had to be brought in to ask them to send out their content—which was very frustrating for the organizer. My suggestion to you is that when you join a summit, be excited about it, send out your content, and do not be one of those people that the planners spend their time chasing after.

Hosting and Co-hosting Webinars

As we talked about earlier, podcasts and video programs are great things to do on your own. Another great thing to do on your own to demonstrate your leadership is to host your own webinar.

Many coaches create what is called a signature system: their own specialized system for how to accomplish something (how to lose weight, how to create a successful relationship, how to get clients, how to write a book that sells, etc.).

To get people to sign up for the signature system, many coaches offer free educational webinars where they give their audience a small taste of the program. The webinar length is usually one hour; half of the webinar is learning about how to do something (for example, five ways to get speaking gigs), and the other half is making an offer for their system (for example, sign up now during this webinar and receive my program for 30 percent off the regular price). The webinar is full of rich educational content that makes the attendees want to learn more and feel they need to sign up for the paid program.

The webinar is heavily promoted online to get many people to sign up, and it usually involves paid social media ads, organic social media posts, and emails. Often the webinar host asks their joint-venture associates to also market the webinar to their email list and social media followers. Webinars are a main online tool to sell paid programs.

In addition to selling a paid program, a webinar also sets you up as an established expert. With all the advertising you are doing and all the emails that are going out, more people will learn about you, and if joint ventures are promoting you, then the joint venture followers also see that you are a prominent person. An established business owner usually only markets a colleague in their industry for two reasons: because they will make large sums of money as an affiliate of the program, and because they believe the colleague is offering a great product. Again, all this promotion makes you the leading authority in your field to both your current tribe and the new people coming into your tribe.

When the webinar goes live and you have your audience joining you, you send out the same signals you do with speaking: you are at the front of the room (this time it's a virtual room), sending out the message of leadership and expertise. The audience will look up to you, take you seriously, and have great respect for you. Many of them will sign up for the paid product you are offering at the end of the webinar, and for those who don't sign up, you have still made a lasting impression. They will be glad to be part of your online community, will look forward to your future educational emails and social media posts, and will want to sign up for future free events. They might not sign up for the product now, but there is a good chance they will sign up at a future date. Another great benefit of your outstanding performance on the webinar is that the participants might refer you to their associates. It's all celebrity marketing at work!

The first time you create a webinar, a lot of people won't show up. If you want more people to show up for the next webinar, you must update it, fix it, and fine-tune it. More people will show up the next time, and even more the time after that. More people will show up as you keep marketing and improving your webinars. After each webinar you host, evaluate it, and ask participants for feedback with a survey. Look at what you did wrong, and figure out what to do right.

If you want to connect with more people in your mastermind and networking groups, why not partner with them and do an educational webinar? Invite them on as a guest where you will both teach on a topic in your industry, or instead of doing joint teaching, conduct an interview.

To receive a huge audience for the webinar, you and the guest need to both get the word out. Getting the word out involves the standard methods that we have discussed. Both webinar leaders' actively engaging in marketing will ensure a huge number of listeners because it results in both lists attending. At the end of the session, if you provide a giveaway, then the attendees will go ahead and sign up for the offer. Assuming that around fifty percent of attendees were not previously on one of your lists, your lists will now have a much larger number of subscribers.

Thus, when selecting a co-host for the program, ensure it is someone who does their part in co-publicity. Most people out there will jump at the opportunity to take part in a webinar, but that doesn't mean they will work hard and share it with others. Co-hosting a webinar involves more than just showing up for it; being a co-host means also producing campaigns for the purpose of getting your fan base to take part in it. You don't want to fall into a trap where you spend long hours of your time on producing and sharing content and your colleague doesn't do their part. When this happens, the co-presenter benefits because your subscribers join their list, but you receive nothing because your co-presenter's followers don't even know about the event, so they can't sign up for your list.

For those who already are part of your community and read the great content that you produce in emails and social media, a webinar will enable them to get to learn more about the person behind all the marketing. They will get a better feel for the real you and what you are all about. For those who are from the guest's database and have never heard of you, once they see you in action providing content of fabulous educational value, they will be amazed by you, will want to sign up for your emails, and will join your social media pages.

Most people subscribe to several email lists and social media pages, making it hard for the owners of the pages and emails to stand out. With a webinar, you get to the front of the crowd, similar to being on stage as a speaker at a meeting. Webinar attendees are impressed that you can team up with another industry leader and lead an event.

Hosting an online program has some similar advantages to speaking at a live event. A reason for the popularity of webinars is the interaction it provides with the audience. Most webinar programs have a chat function where viewers can post questions to the presenters. At the end of the webinar, the presenters will take a few minutes to mention the questioners' names and then answer their questions. The questioners and the rest of the viewers feel like they are talking directly to the hosts, having a conversation with the hosts, and getting to know them on a deeper level; they feel almost as close as being live in a room and face-to-face with the presenters.

In addition to receiving a whole group of new people to follow you online, co-hosting a webinar increases your visibility and demonstrates your influence, expertise, and leadership to both you and the guest's community.

Having Television Spots on News Shows

If you can get on a talk show or news show to discuss your business expertise, I recommend you go for it. Many new people will see you on the show, and being on a TV program will look prestigious and will cause you to gain many new fans and increase your profile. When you share your appearance with your followers, they for sure will be impressed.

One important thing to do is to make sure you get the video and pictures of your time on TV. Many times I see websites where the website owner creates an "As Seen On" section, and they put up the logos of the programs they appeared on to let the visitors to the site know they have been on those different television programs. However, they have no videos or pictures anywhere of their appearance, and they are missing a big opportunity by not having a visual snapshot.

Upload the video to YouTube and Facebook. Share the YouTube link on all your social media channels and the media page of your site. Write a blog post about the experience of going on a television show that has the embedded YouTube video. Send out an email to your list saying, "Did you catch me on X TV show? If not, here's the video, or read all about the experience on my blog at link Y."

Think about how great you will look to your audience when they see the video. Having the video is much better than just telling people with the "As Seen On" section of logos and way more impressive! Business owners often spend time thinking about the content they must produce, and showcasing your live TV program time will give you loads of fresh content that you can use and recycle because you will want to share your experience every so often to wow your audience. Most likely you will get lots of likes, shares, retweets, and comments by showing the video.

Use the awesome photos for social media and emails discussing your experience. Upload the photos to your website. Put a picture of your appearance on your website "About" page and on the media page that discusses your speaking experience and how to contact you for speaking engagements. If you want to get booked for speaking gigs, think how superb you will look to visitors by sharing pictures of your TV show bookings.

If you really want to showcase your celebrity status to more people, put the TV photos as your social media profile pictures and as the headers on Facebook, Twitter, and LinkedIn. People will be awestruck and will make it a point to join your community as they will want to connect with someone who has such a special status.

Are you wondering how to get on news shows? Here's a secret: most people don't just get invited on talk and news programs. To be blunt, it costs a boatload of cash because they have to hire a public relations firm to get booked as guests on these shows. That's why I'm not devoting a large segment of this book to television; it's much easier to get speaking gigs and podcast opportunities without hiring a specialized expensive agency. However, it can be done—it just involves a good budget. If you are new to business or are looking to get to just the six-figure mark, then I recommend that you don't use your budget for television or photos with famous people. Your budget is better spent on using the other tools I am giving. Once you have an established business, are making more than six figures, and want to go to the next stage of multiple six figures or the seven-figure mark, then I encourage you to contact a PR company and take this step. There are tremendous rewards for doing so.

Recap

- Speaking sets you up as a leading authority in your niche.
- Speaking is a primary driver for success as an entrepreneur.
- Choose two to three elements of the speaking online mix, and dive into them.
- To grow listeners for your webinars, podcasts, and video shows, make it a requirement that guests co-promote their appearance of their episode.
- Make sure to always promote your appearances as a guest on podcasts, video shows, and telesummits.
- Promote your webinars, podcasts, and video shows with great graphics because people are visual.
- Online speaking is evergreen—keep sending out your recordings of podcasts and videos.

Chapter Ten

Where to Speak in Person

We are now going to turn to in-person speaking and the avenues to take for getting in front of an audience face-to-face. To become a celebrity, you need to do both online and in-person speaking. I list below four elements of the speaking live mix. I recommend that you start with joining a networking group and speaking at live networking events. Speaking to groups face-to-face gets you even better results than virtual sessions because it gives you more of an opportunity to form a lasting connection with the listeners.

The Speaking Live Mix

- Attending networking events
- Speaking at live networking events
- Sponsoring events

- Creating your own live event

Attending Networking Events

Although it's best to be a speaker at the front of the room, when you are first starting, it might be hard to get these opportunities, so start off by joining one or two chapters of a networking group in your area. There are probably several in your location. I recommend attending one event from each group. Then, when you find the ones that your target market hangs out at and where you have a great connection with the members, join those.

Make sure to introduce yourself to the director because the director usually knows most people in the chapter and is the one in charge of the speaking schedule. As you get to know the members and the director and they see how you are a reliable and professional person, they will be glad to refer your services. If you are providing some free services where the members get to see you in action, then they will for sure want to refer you to others for paid services and will feel comfortable doing so. Business owners don't like giving referrals to someone whom they have never worked with, because they don't know if that person can do the work, and they don't want to ruin their reputation. However, when they know that the person is both qualified and reliable, they love to give referrals.

In addition to attending, be a volunteer. There are many options for volunteering in your local chapter. Work the reception desk, offer a few of your services for free to the director, or sit on the planning board. A graphic artist can design banners for events, a copywriter can write the content for the newsletter, a web designer can help with the website maintenance, a caterer can provide free food for events, and a public relations manager can suggest ways to obtain free publicity.

As you get involved in your chapter, you are increasing your reputation. People get to know and learn about you, and your name will come up in conversations with other members. The idea is that you are meeting other people in the group and becoming more visible. You are thus becoming a celebrity in your own networking chapter.

In addition, now that the director has formed a connection with you, they will respond positively to your request to be a speaker at a future gathering. They have heard your brilliant ideas at the planning meetings and seen your volunteer work and now relish the idea of your taking to the podium.

When I first started my business, I attended some networking events but did not get anywhere. I hired a coach to help me understand what I was doing wrong and to set me on the right path. The coach told me to go to the chapter director and ask her if I could do volunteer work for her in exchange for referrals. The director agreed, and I worked on social media and the website for around six months. After a few months, the director saw my qualifications, and she would refer me when someone was asking for an internet marketing specialist. The clients started to roll in for my business. Her referrals about me sounded great; she told people that Heather did her social media and website and that I was creative and hardworking and an expert in my field. The director told me that the coach who suggested that I do the volunteer work gave very valuable advice because it's much easier for her to give referrals when she knows the person is indeed qualified.

Before I leave the discussion on networking, I want to discuss the elevator speech a bit. While I do emphasize the importance of getting in front of a room as the best way to leverage your efforts, do not discount the elevator speech. It's important—make sure you have a good one. Speaking is not done just on the stage at the front of the room; the elevator speech is also a speech. You never know who you are going to meet at a networking function—the thirty-second intro needs to be the best it can be. Work hard at it, rehearse it, and polish it up constantly.

Speaking at Live Networking Events

Speaking at a live event is a prime way to supercharge your business and is more powerful than appearing on a podcast or a telesummit. When people at networking events see that you are the speaker for the evening, they are automatically impressed with you because it sends a message to them that you are an authority in your field. That message is further enhanced when you give a great presentation of relevant information that will help them in their business. They will for sure remember you as opposed to all the other people whose business cards they collected during the meeting.

Nothing beats a one-to-one connection, and joining networking groups is a must. However, working a room means you meet only a few people for a few minutes with a quick thirty-second elevator speech. Think of how many people you are encountering when you are at the front of the room! While many people in the room might have said amazing and impressive things in their elevator speech, taking to the stage accelerates your efforts as you wow people more and give a twenty-to-thirty-minute speech.

A public speech gets you further than an online event because you are face-to-face with people. Thus, a live talk provides more of an impression and is more memorable. It has a high conversion rate because nothing beats a personal connection. After your speech, many people will go up and talk to you and ask you questions. Even for the people who don't talk to you after the speech, they will still feel more connected with you because they have seen you visually and watched you interact live with other people in front of them. As it's a networking event, you might already know some of the people from prior events, or you might see them again at future events. They will remember your face when they see you in the future and will remember you for sure if you gave a great speech. Attendees will also tell others about you the next time they see you in a room if you gave a speech, such as, "Oh, that's X. I heard her speak at the meeting a few months ago on topic Y. It was a great speech, and I learned a lot." Again, public speaking elevates your status and puts you on the road to prominence.

A well-structured talk is a must! Don't miss this opportunity to shine. There are many courses available to help you prepare a great speech, and I recommend you go sign up for at least one of them. You can also hire a speaking coach. Right now, I will take this time to highlight a few things that your speech must contain.

The first thing to remember is to always answer, "What's in it for them?" (WIIFT). The speech is not about you and how great you are. It's about them—the audience. Most of your presentation needs to be on a great topic full of insightful information and a resource to the audience's needs. To form a connection with the participants, make sure to have a thorough understanding of them, and craft your talk to their interests.

You should for sure include a bit about you, but make it brief. Let them know about you, your experience, and why they need to listen to your presentation. To highlight your skills, discuss how you worked with several people who were facing a situation, how you solved it for them and delivered great results—and now how you are going to share your secret sauce with the audience. Remember, it's about status. You are the expert! Enforce your acclaim by letting your audience know your proficiency, your years in business, some of the successful clients you have worked with, and how you made a difference in the world. The participants will see your prominence and will be impressed—which is the goal. However, don't make your biography too long and all about you. Just remember the basic rule that they did not come to hear about you; they came for your topic.

At the end of your presentation, make sure to include your website link, or send around a sign-up sheet for your irresistible free offer. Your offer can be a free e-book, gift certificate, audio lesson, or private one-to-one session for them to learn more about working with you. You can also mention a paid event or product. This will all depend on your strategy and what you are currently up to in your business. Many of the attendees who listened to your talk will go to sign up for your giveaway or paid product. Being the megastar in the room is the fastest path to clients and delivers staunch results!

Want to continue to make an impact and let the speaking work for you? Communicate to your followers that you will speak at an event. Let them know ahead of time that you will be the keynote speaker, and mention it again once the gathering is over. Take photos of you on the stage to discuss on social media, write a blog post and newsletter article about the experience, and include a photo of you in front of the audience in your emails. Your followers will look at you with fresh eyes and be awestruck with your success.

Don't be shy, and let everyone in your community know—be the powerful person you were born to be!

Sponsoring Events

Many networking groups, summits, and conferences provide attendees the chance for sponsorships. Sponsorships come in the form of exhibit booths, logos on summit websites and a few minutes of speaking to a crowd during the event.

Sponsorships are a great way to increase your visibility, make a great impression, and stand out from the crowd. Your logos and marketing materials will make a huge impression. People will look at you as influential because you spend money on your marketing, and they will make it a point to learn more about you.

Having an exhibitor booth at a conference is a fabulous idea. Your booth will feature your materials, your giveaways, and yourself. People will stop by the booth (especially if you have a great giveaway) and get to know you. It's another way to elevate your acclaim as opposed to just working the room and going up to individuals for conversations. Remember, speeches are done not just from the stage; speeches include the elevator introduction and, in this case, the booth speech. My recommendation is the same for the elevator speech as the booth speech—it's of paramount importance. Do not discount it, and make it supreme.

Getting speaking gigs is difficult at times because it means you have to get the attention of the organizer, and getting your articles accepted by prestigious magazines is hard work because the editor has to agree to your content. But sponsorship will most likely always be a yes because you are paying for it.

Even though you are not on the stage, still take photos of your booth, and if you do get to speak to the crowd as part of the sponsorship package, take photos of you at the podium as well. Again, think of the impression you will make to your social media followers and newsletter readers as they see how you connected with the attendees at the booth and with your speech and how you had the financial ability to sponsor an event. Even if your sponsorship is just a logo, take a snapshot of the logo in the booklet for the conference, and share it with your readers. Let them know how you are out there shining your light!

Creating Your Own Live Event

Taking part in other business events is an excellent way to build your celebrity. However, you don't need to just go to other events. You can host your own event. The same idea as hosting your own podcast and webinar applies here. If you have an event, you can invite the speakers to your event, and of course, you will be the main speaker. The speakers can give their own speeches on stage, or they can be panelists discussing a topic. Think about how if you organize your own event, you will look like a superstar, and you will look even more like an icon when you get other speakers to attend.

Hosting your own live event is a lot of work—much more work than a webinar. The same principles of what was discussed with a webinar apply, though, for a live event. You will want to make sure that the invited participants who share the stage with you also do their part in publicizing the event and selling tickets, as you cannot be the only one filling the room.

Ticket sales involve both organic and paid advertising.

Other steps are sending out many emails to your lists and mentioning the event whenever you are a guest speaker at an online or off-line function. Your invited speakers need to be required to promote the event on their channels. Because of the expense involved and the opportunity it creates for everyone, many summit organizers require participants to sign a contract where they are required, with no exceptions, to do promotional activities. The contract might also require them to sell a certain number of tickets. Too much is on the line to take someone's word that they will publicize the event.

It is much easier to sell your product and services at your own event than elsewhere. People attend the summit, see you in action, and are educated with the awesome information you provide, and thus they will be more enticed to buy your product. It's a much easier format for selling. It's your event, and you are going to provide loads of content and spend a lot of time with your audience. You talk for much longer amounts of time than at other events. You are the celebrity in the room and the one people want to get to know and learn all about.

When you make an offer from the stage at your own event for a paid product or program, many people will want to take you up on it because it's the chance to continue to learn from you and receive more superb content. You are clearly the one who can deliver amazing results for them—they have just seen you in action for a long time. They relish the chance to spend more time in a paid program with this amazing person they have gotten to know. If you are selling a product, your product will produce what it's supposed to. They now trust you based on your educational speeches.

A live summit increases your visibility and prestige because you are face-to-face with people, enabling the opportunity to form a personal connection. Seeing you on stage sets more of an impression than just reading your online content. During the break times of the event, the ticket holders will go up to you for a chat and to get to know you. Their conversations with you will include questions about your talk, general business observations, your insights on your industry, how they can learn more about you, and much more. You will be the leader in the conversations and the one they are looking up to.

As they are getting all this quality information and spending such a large amount of time with you, participants are going to be more impressed with how much of a champion you are and want to buy from you. That's why the offers at live summits are not just for giveaways but for paid programs that have high price tags.

An in-person summit is a fabulous opportunity to bring in the cash and is a door opener to creating a highly lucrative business. If you are just starting out, then I suggest that you don't set up a live event. It will be quite costly and difficult to get speakers and people to fill the seats because you don't have many subscribers. A new business is better off focusing on growing its online community, joining networking forums, working with a speaking coach, launching webinars, and booking as many podcasts shows as possible. Having these objectives will grow your fan base and increase your visibility. You will be a celebrity in your niche with these practices.

Once you have an established business, are making more than six figures, and want to go to the next stage of the seven-figure mark, then having a live, in-person summit is an amazing step to take. It will give you large rewards and explode your business even more.

Recap

- Speaking live sets you up as a leading authority in your niche.
- Speaking live is a primary driver to success as an entrepreneur.
- A public speech gets you further as a leader than an online event because you are face-to-face with people.
- The elevator speech at networking events is also a speech and a way to grow your celebrity.
- Make sure to always promote your appearances as a guest at networking events.

Chapter Eleven

Where to Be a Featured Writer

In addition to public speaking, another great way to increase your celebrity is by becoming a featured writer, and I'm going to discuss four primary ways to publish your writing. The same rules for speaking apply with writing—you don't have to use every publishing location that I'm going to mention. My suggestion is to find one or two that work for you, and then dive into them. Let's say one of them is publishing on article sites—that means submitting an article two to three times a month and not one article every six months. The more places you have an article published, the better, and if it is working for you, then write as often as possible. Remember, though, it is not enough to just submit an article; you need to share your links on social media and newsletters.

If you choose to publish a book, understand that doesn't

mean that you mention the book to your followers sporadically. Once your book is published, dive into promoting it as much as possible with social media, emails, blog posts, podcasts, video shows, and more. Everywhere you go, you need to mention the book for the world to know that you are a published author.

The Featured Writing Mix:

- Publishing your own book
- Publishing on article sites
- Writing your own blog
- Writing small e-books

Publishing Your Own Book

The main benefit of writing a book is that it increases your profile. As the book you have written is full of rich and valuable information, the readers of your book will be impressed with the advice and content that you have shared. They will see you as an expert and leader in your niche. They will proceed to visit your website, sign up for your free offers and follow you on social media. Many new people who have never heard of you will now have heard of you and they will seek you out and want to work with you and hire you.

When you go to an event and hand someone a brochure or a business card, you are perceived as a salesperson and are met with resistance. However, if you hand them a book, you are an expert in your niche. Why the difference? A book gives them the impression that you are an influencer, and they will be intrigued and want to know more about your business. The same thing applies when you put that you are an author in your bio on your website and on the speaker sheets you give to the director of networking chapters whose events you want to speak at.

Being an author elevates you to a level of leadership. It sets you apart from the competition because it puts you above the others in your industry who did not write a book. Even if your competition has more experience, has more social media followers, and has been in business much longer than you, a book lets you stand out from them. It will make people take notice of you, respect you, and want to work with you because you are published and your competition is not.

Once your book is published and available for sale on sites such as Amazon, it's your job to get the word out. You are getting the word out to the marketplace not just for sales of the book (although making a profit is wonderful) but also because readers of the book are likely to want to hire you for services. Once people learn that you are a published author, they will take notice, be impressed with your abilities and consider hiring you, even if they don't purchase the book. Writing a book makes you a celebrity, and here's what you need to do to benefit from your author status.

In the biography section of the "About" page of your website, mention that you wrote a book, and include the graphic of the book cover. On the website home page, place an image of the book cover and include a brief mention that you are the author of this book—this way it's the first thing a potential client will see when they visit your website.

On the speaker sheet that you give to directors of events when you request to be a speaker, mention that you are a published author. You can also impress them by showing the book to them when you see them in person.

Whenever you introduce yourself before speaking,

make sure to mention that you are an author. If you are presenting with slides, put an image of the book there.

At your event booth, put a few copies of the book on the table to show people; displaying the book is a superb way to capture visitor interest and sell some copies. You pique visitor curiosity by demonstrating that you are a writer. Visitors will want to talk with you longer at the booth, which will lead to a discussion of your paid programs and services.

If you are hosting your own podcast or video show, mentioning that you are an author should be part of your bio on your podcast page. When you post guest articles on article sites, make sure to mention there too that you are a published author.

In the bio section of your social media pages, put that you are the author of a book, and give the title. LinkedIn allows a whole section for information on your book, so make sure to add it to your LinkedIn profile. In your social media posts, get the word out that you are an author, and provide a link to where they can purchase the book on Amazon. Social media posts need to have the graphics of the book that clearly show that you are the author of the book on the graphic. You can also put the image on your Facebook, Twitter, and LinkedIn headers to further showcase your celebrity status.

Publishing a book in today's day and age is not hard to achieve and is quite easy if you go with self-publishing. There are loads of self-publishing companies out there, and many of them offer copy editing and publicity services. If you just publish the book, it's very inexpensive. When you add on the additional services of editing and marketing, the fees go up. However, you will want to have a high-quality book in the marketplace that gets great reviews, which is why you might want to consider an editor. If you have many newsletter readers and raving social media fans, then you can rely on your own networks to promote the book. If, though, you have a small following online or you want to get the word out beyond your own networks to grow your lists and get even more sales and customers, then you might want to consider the publicity services that a self-publishing company offers. I recommend you take advantage of this additional marketing, as it will for sure be of tremendous benefit for your company.

Publishing on Article Sites

As I discussed earlier with writing a book, writing sets you apart from the competition and makes you be seen as an expert. Writing articles for premier internet sites and magazines has similar effects as book writing. If you can tell people that you are published in a leading magazine for your industry, think of how captivated they will be. You can even print out the pages of the magazine that your article has been featured in and take them with you to networking events to show people and say, "If you want to learn more about me, here is an article I wrote for magazine X," and then hand them the printout during the elevator speech or at the exhibition booth.

You can also write for article sites and magazines in your niche that are not as prestigious as the leading ones. While it doesn't sound as esteemed as the way writing for a premier one does, it still looks good and reaps benefits. For the not-as-popular magazines, I don't recommend printing out the pages and taking them to networking events; however, there are still methods you can use for them to help you stand out in the crowd. I outline here what you need to do when your article is published—whether for a general or famous publication.

Online article sites usually allow a box for your bio, and that means whenever someone reads your article, they will learn about you—a major benefit. Thus, make sure to always include along with your article your bio, a link to your website, and the location where they can opt in to your giveaway.

A big benefit to submitting your articles to online article sites is that it directs traffic back to your website. Many new people will read your article and be impressed with your expertise. They will want to learn about you and your business and thus will click the link in the biography section. The link in the bio section will bring more traffic to your website.

As I mentioned in an earlier chapter, what a lot of businesspeople do that I think adds great value in setting them up as a leader in their field is that they put on their websites and sales pages an "As Seen On" or "Featured On" section. Here they list the logos of all the places that their articles have appeared, and if they have appeared on any leading podcasts, radio shows, or television shows, they also put the logos in this section. On their website, they have a media page with links to all the online locations where their articles and speaking have appeared.

I recommend that whenever you have an article published that you save the web page where the article appeared as a PDF. Sometimes article sites change their layouts or web hosting, and not everything is moved over from the old site to the new site, leading your link to no longer work in the future. A PDF can be uploaded to a website. This way, when the live link to the online site is no longer active, all you must do is replace the link with the PDF that shows the web page of the blog site of your article.

Your article can also disappear from a respected magazine site, and when this happens, you have nothing to show anymore on your website's media page. This happened to me. I got published on a blog for a leading women's group. A year later, they upgraded their site, and my guest blog post was not transferred over. I did not save the article as a PDF, and I could no longer provide the link to prove to people that I was indeed published with them.

Getting published in a magazine leads to the same process as when you appear as a guest for a webinar, podcast, or live event—you need to get the word out. Every time you have a published article in a magazine or on an article site, mention it on social media and in your newsletter, and include the link to the site where you were published. Let everyone know that you are happy and proud to be featured in this publication! Make sure to include a nice graphic that shows the logo of the site and your image. Remember, people are visual, and they will see the graphic before your words.

Don't mention the achievement just once on social media. When the article is published, make sure to post about your triumph a few times over the first two weeks. Then revisit the post in two to three months. Every four months, remind people that you were published. If the article gets removed from the site, no problem: just put the link to your website where you have uploaded the PDF.

I often work with clients who share once that their article was published and then forget about it. Big mistake! Saying it once is not enough, because many people will not see your post the first time it is out. For your readers to know that you got published, you need to keep repeating it, and for those that did see the post on your success, they most likely will not remember it in four months. Even if they do, they will completely understand why you are mentioning it again.

Writing Your Own Blog

Earlier in this book, I mentioned that I attended a course with a business coach who told the audience that prospects don't care about a blog; they won't read your blog, so don't bother to have one. I completely disagree with her advice (and because it was such bad advice, I made it a point to never purchase her paid programs).

While I agree that a prospect visiting your website is not going to take the time to read every blog post you ever wrote, they are most likely going to check out your blog. They will skim through a few of your articles by looking at the titles and reading a few paragraphs of what you have written. Before someone decides to work with you, they will read a bit of your blog and check out some of your social media posts. If they are impressed with what you have written, it will influence their decision to hire you.

I for sure recommend you have a blog on your website. You should have at least ten posts with great titles and content to impress a visitor to the site.

Now, that is the minimum. What you really should be doing is publishing a new blog post once to twice a month. This way, when someone visits your site, they always see new content. They won't read all your posts, but they will see that you have created recent content and are active on your site.

Here's why it works. A prospect comes to your website and reads a few of your posts. They see by the fact that you have written on a topic several times that you are an expert in the area. While they are not enthralled at the same level as if you are an author of a book, they are still impressed because having a blog means that you have knowledge of an area and that you have enough of that knowledge to write about it. If you have written a bunch of blog posts on your niche topic, then you know a lot and are proficient in your field. Reading your blog makes visitors want to pick up the phone to set up a meeting to discuss your services.

Running your own blog site and having your newsletter are where you can display your expertise. If you are writing helpful and rich content, people will read your content and know that you are an expert in your field. If you have a blog, send out the links to your latest blog post in your newsletter and social media. Let everyone know what you are writing about.

Letting social media followers know about your blog post is another way to showcase your leadership. Make sure to post to your accounts your new blog posts and your old ones. Your fan base will see that you are writing about these topics and will learn more about you and your skills. While the goal is for the audience to click on the link and proceed to your blog to read about the subject, many times they will not. If they don't click but still see the posts about the blog, you still have achieved something.

Writing Small E-books

While free e-books are given away to get subscribers for your newsletters, they, again, show you are an expert.

When I started my business, I wrote three e-books that I gave away on my website. I was offering services in WordPress, Facebook, and SEO, and my three giveaways were on these topics. I wrote them because I wanted to get subscribers to my newsletter who were looking to work with a specialist in these areas. I thought that a great way to get new clients would be to communicate by email with the people who signed up for my free offers. What happened, though, surprised me!

I went to a networking event and exchanged a business card with someone who was looking to hire someone to manage their social media. They went to my website and were impressed that I wrote these e-books. They didn't sign up for any of the books, but they did hire me! They told me on the phone how they were impressed with the fact that I could write these books, and that was one of the reasons for their decision.

I didn't write the books and then just say on my website that I wrote them with a text description to sign up for them. I created nice graphics that showed the title and that I was the author, and I posted them on each page of my website and shared them on social media. As I keep saying, people are visual. I celebrated that I wrote these e-books by sharing the graphics of the books and discussing what they are about. I mentioned how I was the writer, and this showed my expertise because if I can write a book, then I must be proficient. My e-books got people's interest and got business for me.

Recap

- Being an author sets you apart from the competition.
- People are visual, and therefore you must show the graphics of the books and e-books you have written on your website and social media pages.
- Mention that you wrote a book in all your biographies: on your website, social media pages, speaker sheet, and so on.
- Bring your published book to your event booths.
- After your article is published, mention it many times on social media and in your newsletter.
- When a visitor to your website sees that you have written a bunch of blog posts or e-books on a topic, they will know you are proficient in your field.
- Writing small e-books for free is both a great way to grow your newsletter subscribers and show your proficiency in your field.

Chapter Twelve

Case Studies

Over the years, I have worked with a variety of purpose-driven entrepreneurs who have a range of businesses from life coaching to business coaching to public speaking to book writing.

I'm going to discuss how two different clients with two different businesses used their own combinations of the online tools that we discussed in the previous chapters to grow their online prominence, promote their businesses, and drive massive revenue.

Francine

My client Francine is a business coach and strategist and wanted to boost her online presence for profit growth. Francine decided to launch a podcast where every week a guest would be invited to her show. At first the podcast was slow to gain prominence. As her marketing specialist, I would send out many emails to different entrepreneurs inviting them on the show, and many of the emails would not get any response. Eventually, though, as more episodes would air, we saw more emails get positive answers, and guests agreed to make appearances. About a year and a half after the show premiered, entrepreneurs started to reach out to us to be a guest on the podcast. My job involved sending out fewer emails to invite guests because we had a huge list of people who were reaching out to us seeking to be a guest.

As each guest was required to promote their interview, people started hearing about the show, and listeners grew each week. Francine also did her part with promotion. Emails were sent out each week to announce the latest episode, and social media was created for Facebook, Twitter, LinkedIn, and Instagram with information about the guest of the week along with a link to the show. The listener numbers kept growing, and with more listeners came more sign-ups for Francine's programs.

Francine's celebrity status grew. She mentioned prestigious guests who appeared on her show in her emails and social media posts. Visuals that included the podcast name, episode number, a photo of the guest, and the guest's name would accompany the emails and posts. Readers were amazed and saw Francine's leadership in her field, as she was hosting her own podcast on a regular basis and interviewing prestigious members in her industry.

Doing a podcast was not enough to increase Francine's visibility, though. Francine and I felt that in addition to her podcast, speaking would also be a great asset to add to her marketing mix. I reached out to networking groups in her area to let them know about a great speaker and provided them with a speaker sheet that listed her topics and biography. When I first sent out the emails, I received barely any response. However, we did not give up. We kept sending out emails, and eventually we got responses with speaking engagements. As the podcast grew in listeners, more people heard of Francine, and it helped her get speaking gigs.

Francine did not stop with speaking for networking events. Her speaking gigs also included paid sponsorship for events that let her speak on stage, being a guest on other podcasts and webinars, and hosting her own live events.

At every public appearance, Francine always let the audience know about her irresistible free offer and where they could sign up. If the event organizers allowed for it, Francine also told the audience about her paid programs. For paid sponsorship and her own live events, she was of course permitted to mention her paid programs.

With her speeches, Francine would always give an impressive talk to the audience full of detailed and valuable information, and she made sure to follow the 80-20 rule. As Francine demonstrated her knowledge at each event and on each podcast, the audience was impressed with her knowledge and insights and understood that she was a savvy businessperson. Many of them wanted to work with her to grow their own businesses and would proceed to sign up for her free and paid offers.

For every public speaking event that occurred, Francine and I always promoted them in her emails to her lists and social media posts. Followers were impressed at Francine's ability to get in front of an audience and share a topic. As they saw that Francine was invited to speak at many different places, they saw her as an expert in her industry. By sharing the events online, Francine grew her email subscribers and social media followers, which resulted in more sales for her business.

Kara

My client Kara was a relationship coach who worked with women in their twenties and thirties to improve their connections with their husbands and boyfriends as well as gain confidence in themselves.

To build her credibility and get clients for her business, I encouraged Kara to create a Facebook group. Each week Kara would host in the group a Facebook Live conversation and chat that would be focused on a topic. The group members would ask questions, and Kara would warmly and patiently answer their questions. When Kara had a giveaway or paid product that she was offering, she would mention it in her emails, social media pages, Facebook group, and weekly live Facebook group session. Members of the group felt connected to Kara from the weekly Facebook sessions; they saw she was a friendly person and an expert on relationships. Members trusted her because they saw how Kara patiently answered questions that were posted. Women would buy Kara's programs because they wanted private coaching time with her. They felt that she was the one to offer expert advice to help them.

Kara did not host her own podcast but would often make guest appearances on telesummits and webinars where she would talk about relationships and offer giveaways. As listeners saw her in-depth knowledge on marriages and relationships, Kara received a constant stream of sign-ups for her offers and grew her email lists and social media following. The buzz generated by her online appearances grew Kara's prominence as an authority in her field.

Every time Kara knew she would appear on a telesummit or webinar, she made it a point to have me set up the social media posts with links to sign up to attend and graphics of the event for her online community. Many times, her followers would register for these telesummits and webinars. The additional benefit of online promotion was that her audience was very impressed that the organizers sought out Kara's expertise for their summits.

Kara enjoyed writing, so we submitted her articles to many different article sites. In her emails, Kara would post the links to the articles and encourage readers to click the links and read the articles. With each article submitted, Kara mentioned her biography as well as her giveaway encouraging readers to subscribe to her email list. On her website home page, Kara put an "As Seen On" section with the logos of all the article sites where her articles appeared. On Kara's website there was a media page that listed the sites and had links to her articles. The media page also included the titles of the webinars and telesummits that Kara participated in as well as some videos of these events. Sign-ups for Kara's free offers grew from her article contributions to online sites.

Kara knew that she needed to get out there and meet people and could not grow her business just by sitting behind a computer. To get customers, Kara and I looked for events for single people and speed dating sessions in her area where she could be a sponsor. Being a sponsor at these events enabled her to speak live for a few minutes to the group of attendees and hand out her business card to participants by letting them know she was a relationship coach who specialized in helping singles find their soulmate.

For many of the events that Kara sponsored, someone took a photo of her in front of the audience, and the snapshot would be shared on social media along with some content about how Kara enjoyed the experience. Seeing

Kara at different functions impressed her community and let them see her as an elite relationship coach.

Celebrity Marketing Achieved

Both Kara and Francine took different approaches to using celebrity marketing, elevating their status, and leaping to the front of the line for sales. They both chose different areas of the marketing mix to focus on. Their choices were based on areas that they enjoyed working with and what they felt suited their needs and would be the best way to reach their target market. Both Kara and Francine always made it a point to share their appearances with their online communities by mentioning the events on social media and in emails.

Kara loved writing and answering questions, so articles and Facebook groups composed a large focus of her time. The article sites Kara submitted to were where her niche spent their time. As her Facebook group was a group about relationships, it was a place her niche market spent their time. Kara knew that people in relationships are always seeking advice and asking questions, so videos where she could answer questions were the best way to connect with prospects.

Francine liked hosting a show and inviting on guests, so a weekly podcast was where she spent her energy. She liked to go to networking groups and interact with people in person, so she put a lot of time in at live events. Networking groups are where entrepreneurs spend a large portion of their time, and many of the entrepreneurs in these networking groups want to meet experts who can help them with strategies to repair and grow their business. Francine knew that live events were a prime way to get clients.

What both Francine and Kara did was always mention an offer. They got as many people to subscribe to their email lists by using different elements of their marketing arsenal. They knew that someone finding out about them did not always result in an immediate sale but that it does plant the seed, and that is the first step. Kara and Francine understood that staying on the top of their prospects' minds is the way for their business to flourish and to produce income for many years.

Getting someone whom they connected with in a group or webinar or article to stay in touch with them is the first step. The next step is to always send out emails to their list and post on social media to maintain their connections and create raving fans (and the bonus benefit of readers sharing and forwarding their emails and posts). The writing and graphics are top-notch to continue to impress the audience. By doing so, sales that did not come in from the first connection will come in the future.

Recap

- Kara and Francine choices were based on what they felt would be the best way to reach their target market.
- Both Kara and Francine always made it a point to share their appearances with their online communities.
- Even though they used different elements of the marketing arsenal, Francine and Kara always made sure to mention their offer.
- Kara and Francine knew that someone finding out about them did not always result in an immediate sale but that it does plant the seed.
- Kara and Francine understood that staying on the top of their prospects' minds is the way for their business to flourish.
- Both Kara and Francine use top notch graphics to promote their appearances and events.

Chapter Thirteen

Building a Tribe as a Leader and Celebrity

Your Tribe

Your tribe is the people that follow you online on a regular basis. They are regular listeners of your podcast, active participants in your Facebook group, and continual readers of your social media posts and emails. In fact, they are not just reading your content but are looking forward to the next time you say something because they value what you have to say. They have seen how the content you provide for them works and how you are not just all talk. They have taken your ideas and put them into action. They look up to you and see you as a leader.

Many of the members of your tribe are purchasing your products, and many of them have not purchased your offers just once but are repeat customers. They are so happy with how you helped them become a success that they have written testimonials for you and have raved about you to their colleagues.

Building a tribe is another key to success. That is why it is so important to provide top-of-the-line educational content whether it is free or paid for. Only by providing valuable material with great substance will people be impressed with you and want to keep reading your content and head to their credit card to make a purchase.

Establishing a tribe is not a quick process; it takes time, dedication, and hard work. I am now going to share some of the steps to take to build a raving base of fans.

First, people need to learn about you and your business. That means setting up social media pages, providing a giveaway for email sign-ups, and getting those speaking engagements we talked about earlier.

Your followers include everyone who has liked or friended you on your social media pages, subscribed to your email list, watched your YouTube shows, or joined your Facebook Lives. The goal is to make sure that they stick around—which is easy, provided your content excels. Once they stick around, they are your tribe.

Thus, the second objective after you have set up your pages is to provide knowledge to your audience. Share with them educational tips and give resources to them for no charge. By doing so, they will enjoy reading your materials and will stick around for the next set of content that comes out.

Third, share your passion. Talk about what matters to you. Some of the content you share will not be what excites you, but you are sharing it because you feel it is important for your audience to learn. That's great. However, make sure that most of your postings have content that inspires you and what you love to talk about. Authenticity is what sells; people can see through someone who is not sincere, and if you show the audience your true self, they will enjoy being part of your tribe.

People buy from people they like. It's easier to make a sale when the potential customer feels like they know you and have a relationship with you. People purchase from someone they respect, someone whom they want to be like and want to model themselves after.

It's fine to start small. Maybe only a few people have liked your Facebook page and your email list has only a few subscribers. That's okay. If you keep sending out the newsletter and writing those social media posts, the numbers will increase.

Your newsletter list will grow if you have a great free offer, and the readers will stick around if you have great content in your emails. Another amazing thing that will happen is that people who have enjoyed reading your emails will forward them to their colleagues and get them to sign up for your emails. You can also advertise your giveaway to get more sign-ups.

As you go to networking events and connect with associates there, you will see an increase in connections for your pages. You will follow the social media of the members of your networking chapter, and they will reciprocate with you. Make sure that your emails and gifts mention your social media links to get more social media connections. Advertising is another option to take.

A major benefit of building a tribe is that you can tailor your paid programs to their needs. As they follow you, they like your content, and you have the right audience to approach and give your offers. A true tribe leader engages with their audience, collaborates with them, and pays attention to what the audience needs. You find out from your tribe what they want and create products that they want. You learn what the audience needs and then create the products based on their needs. They will be excited to buy what you have to offer, and sales come easily using this approach.

Here are some ways to do the research:

- Send out surveys in emails.
- Ask your community on social media.
- Look at the questions that participants ask during live webinars and Facebook Lives.
- Look at the questions that the audience asks at speaking events.

With my tribe, I noticed that many of the members were out there creating podcasts and getting speaking engagements; however, they were not sharing their success with others. They were hiding their triumphs. I noticed that the people who were posting their celebrity were growing their businesses exponentially.

I saw that getting speaking opportunities was not enough and that my tribe needed to share the dates, graphics, recordings, and more with the world. That's what started the process of writing this book. Without seeing the dilemmas of what my tribe was going through, I would not have published this book.

Who Is a Leader and a Celebrity?

Do not get discouraged by numbers. If your numbers are not as high as other people's, it does not matter. You are still a leader to the people that are following you, and they are still looking to you for materials that provide rich, valuable information.

Someone else out there might have two hundred thousand likes on their Facebook page, and you might have only two hundred likes. Others might have loads of views for their YouTube shows, and you might have only thirty views. Do not get discouraged. You are the leader for those two hundred people on Facebook and thirty people on YouTube. If you are providing top-notch tips on your page, your community is happy to be in your tribe and will read and listen to what you have to say.

While the businesses out there with the two hundred thousand likes are most likely making over seven figures, it doesn't mean that you can't make a decent income with your small number of likes. I have worked with many clients who have prospered online with small numbers. These clients stayed focused on what they were doing with their marketing and did not let the numbers worry them. They continued to make sure that they stayed the course with their marketing arsenal of social media, emails, and speaking. They did not let low numbers discourage them or distract them.

Your educational content is about making a difference for your audience. Your community will reach out to you saying that because they read your book and listened to your podcast, you have changed their lives. You don't need the largest audience for this to happen; it can still happen with a small audience.

A leader is someone who understands that they have a responsibility to the people that look up to them. They might have a small membership, but they know that they must continue on their journey and share valuable information.

By having a brand with a great message and sharing valuable information, you develop trust with your audience. In life, people don't trust you immediately—trust is earned over time. You show people that you are reliable and can be counted on, and then they begin to trust you. It's the same with your online marketing. Over time, as you regularly and consistently post your content, people will develop trust with you. They will take your suggestions and apply them to their business and see that it works. Once they believe in you, they will purchase from you.

People do business with those they know, like, and see as authentic. Regular educational tips that work and address your audience's needs will make them trust you and like you. As you are posting the content over a long period, the audience will feel that they have a relationship with you.

Don't let the numbers discourage you. Just set up a marketing mix and stick to it. Be a true leader to your tribe of followers, and keep getting your message and celebrity out. Provide great information, and mention your speaking engagements, podcasts, giveaways, and paid programs. Over time, the numbers will increase, and your tribe will grow. You will have an audience that loves you and continues to rave about you to their friends, family, and coworkers.

If you are doing what needs to be done, the people who were following you in the beginning with the low numbers will be impressed as your numbers grow. Because they have been part of your fan base for a long time, they are more familiar with you and feel that they have a connection with you. They will remember you when you were starting out and have since seen you prosper. The increase will captivate them, and they will know that you are a true success.

I always get referrals from people who tell others how they remember me when I just started my business as an internet specialist with a small number of social media fans. They say that they have seen me grow over the years to now being a leading business strategist who has a large number of people connecting with me online. I must be an expert in my field if I was able to achieve such great results!

For people who are part of your inner tribe, are reading your newsletter, and are following you on social media but are just waiting until they have the budget to hire someone, you will be first on their mind when you mention to them how you are taking part in telesummits and inviting them to sign up for your free e-books.

That's why it is so important to understand the concept of planting the seed and tribe building. A lot of people in your community will not need your services right away, but many will need them in the future, and when they do, because you provided educational material to them at some point, you will be the one they first consider working with.

The Celebrity of Your Tribe

You are the leader of your tribe—the one at the front of the line whom they are all looking up to. You are a leader who is sharing with everyone educational insights and encouraging your community of followers to buy your paid programs. They look up to you for direction and insight. You want them to know what a success you are and to be impressed, which is why you are mentioning your speaking engagements and showcasing links to your published articles in well-known industry magazines.

You are famous to your audience that follows you. Even if you have a small audience, you are known to them. Although the business with many followers is more famous than you and you are a business with not as many followers, you are still known to your own community. Before you had your own social media pages, newsletters, podcasts, video shows, and speaking engagements, no one had heard of you, but now that you are online and speaking, people have heard of you, even if the numbers are small. Let us say, for example, you have two hundred social media fans and two hundred podcast subscribers, and you spoke twice to a crowd of ten people at each event, that's four hundred and twenty people who have now heard of you. You are the celebrity to those four hundred and twenty people. You are more famous than when there were zero people.

We now come to our full understanding of celebrity marketing.

Celebrity marketing is increasing visibility and showcasing success to your tribe of followers so that your tribe sees your expertise, influence, and leadership and wants to connect with you and do business with you. You attract clients and do not chase them.

You don't have to be famous to everyone in every industry. You are famous in your niche and in your tribe. You have achieved celebrity status where it matters most—in the eyes of the people you want to help. You have found the people who want to work with you and trust you. They have the confidence that you can deliver the results to grow their business and increase their profits now that they have seen you in action.

Showing to the tribe that you are a well sought-after speaker with discussions and amazingly designed graphics of places that you have spoken at (including the podcasts and webinars that you have hosted) will further add to their trust of you. Letting everyone know about your speaking and writing success in leading publications will make you a celebrity to your tribe. By creating your celebrity, you will have raving fans who are engaged with you, excited to work with you, and wanting to buy your products.

Letting people know about your speaking success makes you more visible to your audience. It adds to the great educational content that you are providing and makes the audience more engaged with you. The audience that is engaged with you is what will lead to sales for you. You must be visible to your audience, and you must stand out.

As you build your audience and get your audience engaged, they will like your brand and your message, and as they like you, they are willing and eager to purchase your packages.

With a focus on giving knowledge to others, letting your audience see your authentic self, and showcasing your celebrity success, you are on your way to becoming a world-class leader. When you are a leader who knows how to educate, excite, and connect with an audience, they will turn to you for more of the locked-away paid content.

Recap

- Building a tribe is another key to success.
- Establishing a tribe is not a quick process.
- Your online followers who last are your tribe.
- Building a tribe means being a superior educational resource.
- Authenticity sells.
- Use research to find out the needs of your tribe and create products based on those needs.
- The size of an audience does not determine whether there is a leader. A leader can have a tribe of a few or a tribe of many.
- You are famous to the audience that follows you even if it is a small number.
- Building a tribe involves three areas: giving knowledge, showing your authentic self, and showcasing your speaking and writing success.

Conclusion

My goal with this book was to motivate and empower you by letting you know that you too can be a leader and an influencer and that the strategies are open to anyone as long as they are serious about being successful with their online business and follow the required process. If you apply the course of action that I have set forth throughout this book, then you will be a celebrity in your niche. By pursuing speaking engagements, publishing articles, hosting podcasts, and conducting webinars, you will be an industry leader. By sharing your knowledge and posting your speaking successes, you will have loads of social media followers, email subscribers, and website visitors. A large number of people will be attracted to your message and what you have to offer, and they will want to work with you.

Remember, though, it takes time, and nothing happens overnight. Many business gurus out there talk about how they achieved instantaneous success. I'll say it straight with you—that is utter nonsense. Online marketing means you must keep applying yourself. You must keep mentioning it repeatedly in many different channels, not just once in one channel only. Although it's not rocket science, it still takes a lot of work and a lot of time.

Transforming yourself into a celebrity does not have to mean that hundreds of millions of people around the world know about you. It means that you are famous and known in your niche and that your tribe looks up to you as a leader, likes you, respects you, trusts you, and talks about you to others. They grasp that you are an influencer because the content that you discuss in your marketing empowers and motivates them.

As a business owner, you understand how to publicize success—you have the mind-set that you must share and continually repeat your achievements. You do not hide away, and you do not let your fears, insecurities, and limiting beliefs overtake you. Instead, you conquer your challenges, do what must be done, and develop the mind-set to share your triumphs and go out and tell people how amazing you are. You create a highly lucrative business and make sure your audience sees your light shine!

About the Author

Heather Ross, CEO of Heather Ross Marketing, is a Marketing Visibility Growth Strategist, Business Coach, Automation Marketing Expert, and Infusionsoft Consultant.

Heather grows her clients online and offline profit and visibility by exploding their digital footprint. Since opening her business in 2011, Heather has worked with clients ranging from business consultants, speakers, authors, women's networking organizations, health, wellness and spiritual coaches.

Heather draws on her years of experience and expertise of social media, eCommerce, branding, traditional and celebrity marketing. She uses powerful strategies to deliver practical and profit enhancing tools for her clients to increase their revenue, get in front of larger audiences, attract clients and not chase them, grow their leads, and automate their online programs.

Many of Heather's clients continue to work with her as they have seen the results delivered by having their businesses grow and continuously prosper year after year. Her clients often refer her to other business owners who are looking to achieve similar success.

Heather is known for her passionate and "tell it like it is" straightforward approach. A straight shooter with a fast paced and direct working style, Heather believes in the importance of planning and sticking to timelines to succeed.

Heather loves supporting goal driven, ambitious entrepreneurs, who want to maximize their online marketing and automate their systems. She is an essential part of her clients team to reach their revenue goals.

Heather is the author of e-books: "7 Surefire Infusionsoft Strategies to Grow Your List 10X" and "Content Marketing Explained: Why Your Business Needs Content!" Many of her business building articles have appeared in online publications such as EzineArticles®, ArticleCube, and HubPages®.

Heather is a certified Rapid Results Coach and certified Big Money Business Coach. Heather lives in Toronto, Canada. In her spare time she loves to travel, watch television shows, and movies based on comic book characters.

Thank you for reading! Please leave me a review on Amazon and let me know what you thought!

FREE GIFT

Engineer Your Celebrity Productivity Planner

To thank you for purchasing my book, I have a special gift for you!

A free electronic productivity planner where you can put together your to-do list and action items as you select the components of the celebrity marketing mix and build your business as an industry leader.

To get you closer to achieving your goals, included in the planner are the components of each mix, and tips with advice.

http://www.HeatherRossMarketing.com/celebrity-planner

ADDITIONAL GIVEAWAYS

7 Surefire Infusionsoft Strategies to Grow Your List 10X. Get Ready to Have a Huge List That Has Low Unsubscribes and Produces High Paying Clients

Content Marketing Explained: Why Your Business Needs Content. Get your e-book with everything you need to know about content marketing.

New items are always being added so keep checking back at the website.

http://www.HeatherRossMarketing.com/free-stuff

COMPLIMENTARY SESSION AND WORK WITH HEATHER

30 minute "Business Breakthrough" coaching session.
We'll work together to...

- Create a crystal clear vision for your "ultimate business success" and the "perfect lifestyle" you'd like your business to provide
- Uncover hidden challenges that may be sabotaging the growth of your business and keeping you working too many hours
- Leave this session renewed, re-energized, and inspired to turn your business into a highly profitable, revenue-generating machine that practically runs itself.
  http://www.HeatherRossMarketing.com/complimentary-session

CONNECT WITH HEATHER

- Connect with Heather on Facebook
  http://www.HeatherRossMarketing.com/facebook
- Connect with Heather on LinkedIn
  http://www.HeatherRossMarketing.com/linkedin
- Connect with Heather on Twitter
  http://www.HeatherRossMarketing.com/twitter
- For more free business building tips and additional information about Heather, go to
  http://www.HeatherRossMarketing.com

www.ingramcontent.com/pod-product-compliance
Lightning Source LLC
Chambersburg PA
CBHW071001050326
40689CB00014B/3437